CONTENTS

HOW GOOD IS YOUR LIBRARY?
A REVIEW OF APPROACHES TO THE EVALUATION OF LIBRARY AND INFORMATION SERVICES

BY JOHN BLAGDEN AND JOHN HARRINGTON
CRANFIELD INSTITUTE OF TECHNOLOGY

1 INTRODUCTION

This review arose out of a proposal made to Aslib and the British Library R & D Department for the development of a multi media publishing project covering the whole area of library and information service evaluation.

This review and the attached annotated bibliography is intended as the first stage of this project. It should be emphasised however that it is hoped that the review and bibliography will be useful to library and information managers irrespective of the outcome of this publishing proposal.

2 ARRANGEMENT

Abstracts of all publications on evaluation cited in this review will be found in the annotated bibliography following this article. The abstracts are arranged in alphabetical order of the first author's surname and where more than one item is cited by a particular author the latest work will be cited first.

3 SCOPE OF THE ARTICLE AND BIBLIOGRAPHY

An online literature search was conducted from 1982 onwards and the two 'core' databases searched were Library and Information Science Abstracts and Information Science Abstracts. It was considered appropriate however to extend the search to include significant developments (especially in the methodological area) in education, management and sociology. Searches again from 1982 onwards were conducted on ERIC, Sociological Abstracts and Economic Literature Index.

The searches were seeking publications that

i   advanced our knowledge of the conceptual basis for performance assessment

ii   described innovative methodology for undertaking studies

iii   reported interesting reliable results

The focus was very much on recall as we wished to avoid missing any significant items. This caused some difficulties and we encountered two problems in particular

i   the imprecision with which authors used such terms as cost benefit analysis, cost effectiveness, etc.

ii   the difficulty of being able to distinguish between literature assessing the **overall** performance of a library system (the focus of our study) and studies that examined specific services.

The focus was not only on **overall** performance but also concentrated on **outputs** and **outcomes**. Allred (1979) somewhat simplistically describes output as the end product of the service but perhaps it should be more specifically defined as any client exposure to any service component. Outcomes should be defined in terms of what effect or impact this exposure has on the client. This is at odds with the recent manual produced by Griffiths & King (1989) who describe output measures in such areas as book processing, cataloguing and binding.

This review therefore excluded such studies as the efficiency of cataloguing throughputs unless an attempt was made to relate such studies to corporate goals and/or user needs. Because the focus is on outputs and outcomes the problems of establishing the costs of supplying library and information services have only been considered in outline. Similarly the impact of new technology has also been largely ignored although such developments as CD ROMs, electronic publishing, microcomputing, distributed processing and more user friendly search protocols could lead, as Beckman (1987) and Thompson (1983) suggest, to the library being bypassed. Our defence for omitting this important area is that libraries may be bypassed in the future but this is by no means certain. In addition many of the concepts and techniques outlined here can equally be applied to the situation described by Lewis (1980) in his milestone doomsday scenario paper in which he suggests that the days of the librarian intermediary may be numbered.

Regrettably the search excluded foreign language material given the restricted time available for the project. Although the online searches commenced with 1982 seven other major sources were used to complement the results of these searches: Allred (1979); Blagden (1980); Brockman (1984); Goodall (1988); Kania (1988); Lancaster (1977); Layzell-Ward (1982); and Powell (1986). From these a number of significant papers predating 1982 were discovered, and these have also been included in the bibliography.

4 PERFORMANCE ASSESSMENT CONCEPTS

We have now had over a decade of cost cutting throughout the library and information services sector and much of the interest in this area has resulted from these economic pressures. Certainly it would seem logical as Blagden (1980) suggests that unless you are able to demonstrate that specific benefits have been achieved as a result of investing in any library or information system then the validity of that initial investment decision will increasingly come under attack. The interest in this area has also been sharpened by the increased emphasis on applying management principles and techniques to information and library services.

The heart of the management approach is of course to define objectives, develop methods of meeting those objectives and to assess how effective this whole process is. Schauer (1986) perhaps somewhat unrealistically argues that goals of libraries must be expressed in such specific terms that changes are **both observable** and **measurable**.   Monitoring performance is an integral part of good management and is really undertaken for two reasons:

i   to convince the funders and the clients that the service is delivering the benefits that were expected when the investment was made

ii   as an internal control mechanism to ensure that the resources are used efficiently **and** effectively.

These differing evaluative viewpoints are neatly encapsulated in the diagram quoted in Cronin (June/July 1982).

	User	Management	Sponsor
Cost			
Effectiveness			
Benefits			

Note: See below

The framework suggested by Vickery (1973) is also a useful starting point in any discussion:

i   the economic efficiency of a system, ie the degree to which it minimises cost in achieving an objective

ii   the effectiveness of a system, ie the degree to which it achieves its stated objective and

iii   the value of a system being the degree to which the system contributes to user needs.

If the value can be expressed in monetary terms and compared with cost then this becomes a cost benefit analysis. Value as a concept is fully explored in the monograph by Taylor (1986) and he has produced over 20 very useful definitions of how information and library systems add value and it frequently appears to be the case that the terms value and benefit are treated as synonymous terms. Schauer (1986) argues that the best indicator of value is usage but Blagden (1988) maintains that the focus should be on beneficial usage which then becomes a somewhat circular proposition.

The concept of cost benefit analysis will be treated in more detail in our next section but it should be noted here that although cost benefit data is difficult to develop, cost **per** benefit is not.

Orr (1973) in his important paper makes the interesting distinction between how good the library is and how much good the library does.

	QUALITY		VALUE
Resources	Capability	Utilization	Beneficial effects
	Demand		

Note: see below

Note: Diagrams on this page reproduced by permission of Aslib

Buckland (1982) explores this concept of goodness in a review of the various hypotheses that Orr developed.

Dumont (1980) argues that there is great confusion over definitions of effectiveness in that it can mean user satisfaction or efficient use of resources in achieving objectives or even job satisfaction of library staff. Dumont advocates a contingency approach by defining library effectiveness in terms of each library's level of ability in responding to its own unique situational and environmental constraints. She also claims that a systems approach can overcome some of the definition problems that this area presents, as do Dervin and Clark (1987).

A variation on the systems approach is the one suggested by Brember (1985) based on the Checkland soft systems methodology. The approach here is to build up a model and then compare this with what is happening through the development of a 'rich' picture of the library services. How this picture is created is fully described by Brember and Leggate (March 1985). The heart of the Checkland methodology is the CATWOE analysis where

C = Customers
A = Actors - those who undertake the activities to make the system work
T = The transformation process
W = Weltanschauung world image
O = Owner who has the power to cause the system to cease existence
E = Environmental constraints

Lancaster (1977) provides a useful tangible set of criteria for assessing the benefits of library and information services.

i   Cost savings through the use of the service as compared with the costs of obtaining needed information or documents from other sources.

ii   Avoidance of loss of productivity (eg of students, faculty, research workers) that would result if information sources were not readily available.

iii   Improved decision making or reduction in the level of personnel required to make decisions.

iv   Avoidance of duplication or waste of research and development effort which either has been done before or has been proved infeasible by earlier investigators.

v   Stimulation of invention or productivity by making widely available the literature on current development in a particular field.

Curiously, earlier in the same book, Lancaster appears to perceive libraries as being primarily in the document delivery business and should be judged by this criterion alone. Dumont (1980) like many other commentators argues that one cannot use a single criterion to judge performance. Lancaster (1977) however takes Armstrong (1968) to task for claiming

"In the case of a farmer who borrows books on how to construct a house, the house built is the real product. This approach is completely unacceptable. The library has served its function adequately if it has a supply of good, readable, up-to-date books on how to construct a house and can make these available at the time the user needs them. Whether or not the reader does construct the house is governed by a myriad of

factors that are completely beyond the control of the library. Moreover, of all these factors, the availability of suitable reading materials is likely to be one of comparatively minor importance. Assume, for example, that user A and user B come to a library seeking books of house construction. Both borrow materials that they consider suitable for their present purposes. A subsequently builds a house, B does not. It is doubtful that anyone could say that the library succeeded in the first case and failed in the second. It could, however, be legitimately claimed a failure if user B was unable to find suitable materials in the library at the time he needed them. The attitude adopted in this book (Lancaster's) is that a library can only (our emphasis) be evaluated in terms of whether or not it is able to provide the materials sought by users at the time they are needed. What the user subsequently does with these materials is completely outside the librarian's control (and, some users might say, none of the librarian's business)."

It is not appropriate here to pursue the question of reader privacy and the related issue of data protection. Suffice to say that in any study of library users the ethics of protecting respondents' anonymity would apply. The authors of this review would however take issue with Lancaster (1977) that libraries should be assessed **purely** in document delivery terms (important though that is) whilst of course accepting that there are many other factors which need to be considered when deciding what constitutes a beneficial outcome. An obvious example here would be of a library and information service supporting a local authority engaged in house design, construction and maintenance. Surely the funders and managers of such a service would and should be very interested in what contribution information and publications supplied by the library directly made to the construction of good quality low cost housing?

5 COST BENEFIT ANALYSIS

Do the costs justify the benefits is what cost benefit analysts seek to determine. Wolfe (1974) emphasises that

"Whilst profit maximising firms will consider only the returns and costs borne by them welfare maximising public decisions must include in the decision calculus the external or spillover benefits and costs that accrue to other parties."

However most library and information services **including** those in the private sector operate in a non market environment as a 'free' service. Interestingly Melrose-Woodman (1974)* in a survey of how UK companies charge for overhead services concludes that there is certainly no strong trend towards internal markets in the private sector.

J L King (1983) and Schauer (1986) identify a number of approaches to cost benefit analysis:

i   maximise benefits for a fixed cost

ii   minimise costs for a given level of benefits

iii   maximise the ratio of benefits over cost

---

*   Melrose-Woodman, J E. Profit centre accounting: the absorption of central overhead costs. (1974) Management survey report No.21, British Institute of Management

iv   maximise the net benefits (present value of benefits minus present value of costs)

v   maximise the internal rate of return

Ratchford (1982) attempts to apply the concept of cost benefit analysis to consumer purchasing behaviour and information seeking. Clearly the rational purchaser will always be attempting to develop effective trade-offs between searching for more information to improve purchase decisions and the 'cost' of so doing. Layard (1972), Wolfe (1974) and Ratchford (1982), and many other commentators, all emphasise other important considerations when conducting cost benefit analysis:

i   the relative valuation of costs and benefits occurring at different points in time, the problem of time preference, and the opportunity cost of capital; and

ii   the valuation of costs and benefits accruing to people with different incomes.

In the next section a review is made of some of the attempts that have been made to assign monetary values to the benefits obtained from using a library. White (1985) with some justification is very critical of these attempts and certainly too much emphasis has been placed on the search for these monetary values. Nevertheless there will always be pressure to justify benefits in cash terms and the cost benefit analysis methodology can also be useful in providing a more coherent evaluative framework even when benefits are not assigned specific cash values.

6 APPLYING MARKET FORCES

A number of recent government papers in the UK, such as the Cabinet Office (1983), Office of Arts and Libraries (1987), the Green Paper on Financing Public Library Services (1988) and a subsequent statement by the Minister for the Arts (Office of Arts and Libraries, 1989), have suggested that libraries should perhaps become more entrepreneurial and charge for services. Arguments about assessing benefit can then be reduced to equating benefit with a willingness to pay, ie if the revenue exceeds the cost then the service justifies its existence. Davison (1988) is however very sceptical of the ability of academic libraries to generate income levels of the order of 20-25% of total income suggested by government. He warns however that whether these figures are achieved or not the government will 'hypothecate' that such sums have been achieved and will reduce funding on the basis of that assumption.

It is rare however for users to be charged for **all** library services although the paper by Griffin (1980) describes such an attempt. Generally where charges are applied they are applied selectively and library managers will still have to justify the bulk of library services by some other means than willingness to pay.

Even with those services that do recover **all** of their costs this market approach does still pose some problems as Flowerdew and Whitehead (1974) point out

"Willingness to purchase an information service at a particular price only reveals that the purchaser values the information at that price or more. The price may therefore not measure the full benefit to the purchaser".

There is also the general problem of the attitude of society towards information as Wolfe (1974) again indicates

"What are the forces that have caused the provision of total secondary information services to come largely into non-private hands. Partly these forces are historical; the information field has to some extent developed out of the public library service. The existence of free information provision in some areas and the constant growth of the scope of such provision must necessarily cause any private entrepreneur to hesitate before launching an information agency."

Libraries in this country and elsewhere have largely not charged users directly for their services. This historic factor may well therefore depress any prices that the cost benefit analyst might determine **even when the service is highly valued** by users.

Norton (1988) however argues that with budgets shrinking and pressures to use expensive new technology, libraries have no choice but to move into income generation. The Library Association has produced a useful analysis of the roles of the public and private sectors in the UK (1987) in an attempt to provide input to a coherent national information and library policy as does Durrance (1987) for the USA.

7 SHADOW PRICING

This factor (why should I pay for a service that has always been free?) may even depress attempts to develop shadow prices for services and a fuller discussion of **shadow** pricing concepts can be found in Mishan (1988). The heart of the problem of allocating shadow prices to services where real money does not change hands is that what people are prepared to pay is not the same as what people **say** they are prepared to pay. Wolfe (1974) emphasises this when he states that

"Economists have in the past been reluctant to rely upon surveys of consumer expressed preferences".

Lancaster (1988) refers to the concept of net value which he defines as what users are prepared to pay for information (but not actually pay) less what it costs to supply that information. Shadow prices or shadow values have been assigned by asking users how much of their time has been saved by using a library and information service. The value of this time was calculated on the basis of average salary data and this, it was argued, demonstrated that the cost of the library was more than justified by the value of these supposed time savings. Blagden (1980) pointed out some of the weaknesses of this approach

i   use of libraries is in 'marginal' time, ie lunch hours, and may not be a genuine time saving

ii   small time savings are, according to some economists, worthless

iii   it assumes the information supplied was of value without providing evidence to support the assumption

iv   the user costs of using the service are frequently ignored in such studies

v   users cannot answer the question how much time was saved in general terms and may not be able to answer it even in specific terms

vi   it assumes that all these time savings are translated into improved productivity

Blagden (1980) also reviewed a large number of studies that had used time saved data to justify the investment in the library without apparent awareness of these deficiencies. Warden (1981) reports the use of a similar approach in which she asked users to estimate how long it would have taken them to complete a manual search as compared with the computerised search completed on their behalf by library staff. Again significant time savings are claimed: 84% of the 77 respondents indicated that equivalent manual searches would have taken days or would not have been undertaken at all. It is still difficult to envisage how respondents can produce credible answers to these questions.

Perhaps a better way of proceeding is the one also suggested by Warden (1981) when she asked respondents *"Was the search worth the cost?"* The answers to this question are of course purely subjective but avoid these somewhat dubious attempts to put monetary values on the supplied information.

The danger with methodologically suspect approaches like this is that if the case for the library is conducted solely in these terms then senior management are likely to be unconvinced, and following on this perhaps assume that there is no justification for the investment at all.

8 CLOSING PART OR ALL OF THE LIBRARY

Cost benefit analysis is often used to evaluate alternatives such as locations for a new major airport, eg the Roskill Commission Report*. In terms of library investment it is rarely a case of either investing in or closing the library but rather a question as to what degree of investment is justified, perhaps using the cost benefit framework developed by King & Screm (1983).

Blagden (1975), in a rather limited study, tried to simulate the conditions that would apply in a 'libraryless' environment. He took a sample of information requests which had already been serviced by an in-house library and compared these 'answers' and the time taken by using only external sources.

Another variation on closing the library is contracting out, which is specifically mentioned in the Government's recent Green Paper on financing public libraries (1988), and Sparrow (1988) reports that the British Library, for example, is comparing the costs of organising conservation on an in-house base with that of contracting the process out to the private sector. Contracting out of services will soon become a discretionary option in the UK, assuming that the planned legislation materialises.

9 OBJECTIVES

Pricing of library services and the use of market disciplines is a **means** of regulating access to library services. It is argued here however that this a **means** and not an end in itself. The question of what the purpose of all this activity is still needs to be resolved. Zachert (1986) maintains that there still has been little effort to relate library activities to the impact they have on corporate objectives.

---

* Commission on the Third London Airport 1970/71 (Chairman Lord Roskill)

Cronin (June/July 1982) and Schauer (1986) also emphasise that if this is to be achieved then these objectives must be specific and meaningful. For objectives to be meaningful it is argued that there must be some way of assessing whether they have been achieved or not.

This of course lies at the heart of the problem as Hardy, Yeoh and Crawford (1985) make clear in a review of medical libraries in US hospitals. They point out that the need for libraries is not self evident and it is difficult to refute the proposition that very few patients would be hurt if libraries were to close. Saving lives or reducing the period of hospitalization are the overall objectives of these libraries and the hospitals they serve, but are these objectives meaningful in performance assessment terms? Unfortunately Hardy, Yeoh and Crawford pose interesting questions without providing any answers.

10 LIBRARY STAFF

Although setting objectives was always seen as an integral part of good management in the late 60s this concept was relaunched under the management by objectives banner. What was new here however was the systematic linking of objectives to staff performance appraisal. Both Ifidon (1986) and Dumont (1980) emphasise the importance of performance appraisal of staff in the context of overall library evaluation. Early writers on management by objectives were quick to point out that there can often be a conflict between corporate goals and individual aspirations.

Another aspect of staff performance is how productive library staff are. Hayes, Pollack and Nordhaus (1983) use an econometric model based on the Cobb Douglas function to assess the productivity of US research libraries. Williams (1988) uses traditional productivity assessment techniques to determine how labour efficient libraries are in producing services and products for customers. In both cases however these are a measure of staff efficiency and do not address the question as to whether these services are effective in meeting user needs and/or supporting corporate goals.

11 MARKETING APPROACHES TO MEETING CLIENT NEEDS

All professions will claim that they are client led and the library and information profession is no exception to this. However Taylor (1986) maintains that our preoccupation with technology has tended to obscure this and he re-emphasises the need for a user driven approach as the focus for evaluation. He suggests the development of a value added model but admits that such models currently lack a predictive capability.

Line (1974) in a useful paper explores the range of client requirements by defining:

i   needs as what an individual ought to have

ii   wants as what an individual would like to have

iii   demand as what an individual asks for

iv   uses as what an individual uses.

Needs, wants and demands are further explored in the extensive review of the application of marketing to public libraries by Smith (1983).

The problem with Line's definition of use is that it is often equated with delivery, eg because a book is borrowed doesn't mean that it is read (ie used). Taylor (1986) and Blagden (1988) review the concepts of use in greater detail.

Clarke and Stewart (1985) argue that local authorities should ask are they providing what the customer wants? The authority may still wish to ask are we providing what the customer **needs**, but they point out that the second question must be grounded in the understanding provided by the answer to the first question and cannot be answered by the authority **alone**. The authority that tries to answer the second question without regard to the first does not provide a service **for** the customer but to the customer. The question of need is further explored in the National Consumer Council report on UK public library services where they emphasise that need is very much influenced by prior expectation.

Meeting customer needs (wants?) lies at the heart of the marketing approach adopted by commercial organisations selling goods and services. Zachert and Williams (1986) and Smith (1983) review how these concepts could be applied to library management problems.

In defining the 'market' (potential user community) that the library is attempting to meet, the market needs to be divided, and this is known as market segmentation. Segmentation is necessary because as Kuehl (1973) points out

"User audiences who in total may exhibit heterogeneous use patterns and utility preferences must be classified and clustered into relatively homogeneous use segments, if the marketing concept is to be operationalised".

This point is underlined by Silvey (1976) in the broadcasting context when he states

"In so far as the size of the audience is a measure of a broadcast's success, it is not its absolute size that matters, but how nearly its size approaches the targets aimed at".

Marketing has traditionally segmented markets on either a geographic basis or by employing various demographic characteristics such as age, sex or income, but in both cases product marketing analysts have found that these are generally poor predictors of consumer behaviour.

Haley (1968) describes an approach whereby it is possible to identify market segments by causal factors rather than descriptive factors, which he calls benefit segmentation. The belief underlying this segmentation strategy is that the benefits which people are seeking in consuming a given product are the basic reasons for the existence of true market segments. Smith (1983) discusses how the concept of market segmentation might be applied to public libraries and, like Haley, supports the idea of benefit segmentation.

Vickery and Vickery (1987) review the whole area of use and in so doing reveal that a large proportion of library use is accounted for by a small number of users. Emery (1987) has recently completed some further research which supports these findings in which he uses consumer repeat buying models developed from consumer marketing to assess market penetration. Clark (1983) maintains that typically 5% of borrowers will account for 30% of all transactions.

Brookes (1985) took data from a number of information studies to explore statistical aspects of whether it is valid to regard recorded use over a short time scale as true random samples on which future usage could be predicted. Blagden

(1980) attempted to apply the concepts of market penetration and impact (effect on client) in two special libraries. These two concepts 'to whom and to what effect' are also identified by Taylor (1986) as having crucial importance in trying to assess the added value that library systems confer on their users. Clark (1983) describes a technique for determining who borrows and how much over a period of time and claims that this technique can give more accurate market penetration data.

12 UNOBTRUSIVE TESTING

The question of trying to simulate and then assess client interactions with the library service has been used extensively in the assessment of public library reference services and is known as unobtrusive testing. Although they are only used in this library service area they have been included here because it can be argued that client interaction with the service should be an important starting point for evaluation. It should be noted that Hernon and McClure (1987a) suggest that this technique could be used more widely.

Unobtrusive testing, or unobtrusive measurement, is a 'qualitative' based method of performance evaluation which has attracted a great many conflicting opinions regarding its validity and reliability. The origins of the technique date back to Webb's (1966) review of the theory and utility of unobtrusive measures for social science research. Since this time it has been used extensively by library researchers to determine the quality of library reference services. It invariably involves the use of trained enquirers or proxies to ask questions (for which answers have been predetermined) of library staff members who are unaware that the service is being evaluated. Note however the survey conducted by Van House and Childers (1984) which actually used pre-existing written records of reference transactions.

In the twenty or so years since Webb's work, there have been a considerable number of studies employing unobtrusive tests designed to assess the ability of reference services to provide accurate answers to short factual and bibliographical questions. A selection of the more recent of these includes Gers and Seward (1985), Birbeck and Whittaker (1987), Thompson (1987), Williams (1987) and notably Hernon and McClure (1987a). The results obtained from unobtrusive testing have generally shown remarkable consistency. Hernon and McClure's summary of these findings suggest that reference staff provide 'half-right' answers, in that between 50-62% of the questions are answered correctly; spend an average of no more than five minutes per reference question; experience problems in conducting reference interviews and implementing effective search strategies; and fail to provide referral to questions on occasions when they are unable to provide answers.

According to Hernon and McClure (1987a) the main advantage of unobtrusive testing is that it provides a means to gather data from the perspective of library users, whilst avoiding subjective assessments about the quality of reference services. They also suggest refinements in the methodology which enables the technique to relate outputs to inputs in order to compare the number of correct and incorrect responses to general institutional or organisational variables. Further evidence to support the view that unobtrusive testing does have advantages over other evaluation techniques has been provided by Weech and Goldhor (1982) who in a pilot study demonstrated that libraries performed slightly, but statistically significantly, better on obtrusive tests (ie where the library staff are aware of being tested) than on an unobtrusive one; and suggested this as partial confirmation of the biasing effect of obtrusive tests.

However the significance attributed by Hernon and McClure (1987a and 1987b) to their so-called 55% rule (correct answer fill rate as an output measure) and their portrayal of academic and public library reference services in a state of crisis has provoked a storm of reaction in the literature which has questioned the reliability of unobtrusive testing and the validity of resulting judgements. Hernon and McClure (1987a) do acknowledge that there are indeed limitations inherent in unobtrusive testing. For example, it requires:

i   careful procedures for administration of test questions and careful selection, training and supervision of the proxies.

ii   careful selection of the questions, which should ideally be approved by professional reference librarians before use.

iii   the assumption that libraries do maintain a 'basic reference collection' so that questions should if possible be answerable from more than one source.

iv   that unobtrusive testing does not take into account random variables, such as time of the day, etc, which might adversely affect the ability of staff to answer questions. The test will therefore indicate the quality of a service at a particular time. Hernon and McClure therefore stress the need to repeat data collection over a period of time.

Critics of Hernon and McClure's faith in unobtrusive testing, such as Childers (1987), Schumacher (1987) and Bailey (1987), have raised other potentially serious objections. Childers in particular expresses fears concerning the assumptions required when applying the findings of unobtrusive testing to the reference function generally. He points out that unobtrusive tests have almost exclusively so far relied on short factual type questions which are easy to pose without variation and make it easier to control the interaction with the responding librarian and facilitate consistent judgement of the answers. This type of query, as Schumacher and Bailey both note, represent only one part of the reference function, and one which will not necessarily define the whole of the reference process. Van House and Childers (1984) suggest that the criteria by which answers are evaluated depend on the researchers' beliefs about the completeness of answers and, for example, whether the objective is to answer the question using all, including external, sources or whether the search stops at the library doors. Hence the view of the experimenter may not coincide with the library's formal or informal norms. Van House and Childers (1984) also express concern that unobtrusive testing can be relatively expensive and time consuming and thus not an activity that a library will undertake frequently or easily. On this point compare the conclusion of Hernon and McClure (1987a) that cost and time factors *are not excessive for large and well funded libraries*. Finally some critics still have reservations about the ethics of unobtrusive testing whereas Hernon and McClure (1987c) suggest that, providing research is properly conducted, ethics have become a non-issue.

The response of Hernon and McClure (1987c) to their critics that the acknowledged limitations of unobtrusive testing does not invalidate their conclusions, reflects comments which can be levelled at other performance measures in that unobtrusive testing, like other input or output measures, should not be viewed as a complete solution to evaluation but is one of a range of methods which can, if used efficiently, contribute useful information on the performance of library services.

13 ATTITUDES OF USERS AND NON USERS

Attitudes will influence user assessments of services but, as Line and Stone (1982) comment, measuring attitudes is a complex business and the Newcastle upon Tyne (1985) library service report that

"The subjective perceptions of a service or of a feature of local authority activity bear no necessary connection to that service's or authority's objective performance efficiency or success. A good service assessed by any objective standard might forever be unfavourably perceived because expectations are inappropriate. Indeed some services might always be perceived unfavourably, eg statutory aspects of child care."

Carley (1988) also reports the difficulty of relating client satisfaction to efficiency or effectiveness and points out that respondents can be dissatisfied with a perfectly adequate service because of a variety of unmet needs which the service was never designed to meet.

Another problem with attitude studies is that users rarely have strong views about libraries and therefore one needs a sensitive measuring instrument to tease out these differences. Totterdell and Bird (1976) demonstrate this very clearly when they show that there is little difference between users and non users in their attitude towards public libraries. D'Elia and Rodger (1987) try and establish whether there is a rational base for user behaviour through an extensive survey of twenty US public libraries. They conclude that their results corroborate earlier findings that it is impossible to generalise on user behaviour patterns. Brember (1985) makes an important point about library staff attitudes. He maintains very active users (who account for a high proportion of all use) can distort the perceptions of library staff about the whole user community and thus obscure the needs of both the less active user and the non user.

14 OUTCOMES

Blagden (1988) maintains that performance assessment should be based on what users actually do rather than what they say they do. He argues against general attitude surveys although they can clearly be useful if the results are favourable in political terms. Blagden (1988) maintains that when questioning users they should be asked about **specific** transactions rather than requesting generalised assessments of the library or even a specific service. This is at odds with the recent manual by Griffiths and King (1989) which recommends asking users such questions as how satisfied are they with reference services.

This was one approach that Blagden (1980) took in the context of assessing the performance of two special libraries. It was also the approach adopted by Stone (1983) who interestingly also recorded prior expectations of utility of documents requested through interlibrary loans and then compared these with ratings of the documents usefulness after they had been received. Both Blagden and Stone appear to demonstrate that at least 70% of all material supplied to users is beneficial. The unresolved question is whether that 70% is good or bad? Both Stone and Blagden were concerned with assessing how effective the services were in delivering useful items. They did not deal with the benefits that libraries can confer on their customers through browsing and serendipity.

The methodological difficulties of assessing browsing are outlined by Ayris (1986). It is important that evaluation does not take too mechanistic a route, ie reader asks a question which is answered by a book delivered by the library. Taylor (1986) also maintains that there is this danger that

"In general our systems (narrowly conceived as specified formal processes) have evolved to answer questions rather than address problems. Questions are compromises. They are only part of the larger problem situation. Questions require answers. That is to say questions are satisfied by the most precise chunks of information we can provide. Users however are not interested in just receiving answers to questions but rather in addressing problems. Problems require clarification, resolution and perhaps even solution."

15 INTER LIBRARY COMPARISON

One way of answering the question as to whether a library is good or bad is to try and conduct controlled comparisons between similar types of library. Dyer and O'Connor (1983), for example, suggest ranking libraries by a scoring system.

The application of this technique to libraries in the UK however has been primarily due to the work of the Centre for Interfirm Comparison, whose first report for the British Library on public libraries appeared in 1981 (Centre for Interfirm Comparison 1981).

The information provided in these comparisons takes the form of cost-structure ratios to indicate resource allocation by type of expenditure; functional expenditure ratios to show expenditure priorities on various library functions and services; cost/output ratios to relate resources used to work done in various activities; and background information on the characteristics and methods employed by libraries to facilitate the interpretation of the data produced. By enabling the calculation of unit costs it is suggested that the comparison might help to reveal that one library may have proportionally higher unit costs than another.

However, a number of criticisms (Moffatt 1983) have been levelled in the literature which seem to question the validity of the technique. These include reservations concerning the possible misuse or misinterpretation of the data; inconsistencies in data collection techniques (such as methods used to calculate library staff time) and definitions of output measures between the participating libraries make it difficult to guarantee that like data is in fact being compared. The existence of additional factors such as organisation structure, geographical location and history all affect outcomes, while the comparison provides no actual indication of service quality. Certainly without output measures that are standard across participating libraries and the addition of utility, benefit and quality considerations, the concept of inter-library comparison will be regarded as being of rather limited value, and library managers may be reluctant to invest time and therefore resources in participating in such schemes.

16 COSTING

Inter library comparisons, as has been made clear, have primarily focussed on comparing costs of various activities conducted in groups of libraries. Although this review has concentrated on the benefit side of the cost benefit equation it was considered appropriate to also briefly review the area of costing.

Despite the growing body of literature on costing and library economics in the last twenty years, there has been only a very slow progress towards some consensus regarding the appropriate body of theory, and an apparent reluctance in practice to employ the supporting techniques of costing, accounting and performance measurement. Indeed this is a point firmly made by Roberts (1982) in one of the most significant recent contributions to the literature. Libraries do seem to have developed weak financial and management accounting systems compared to conventional business enterprises and, in spite of the need to justify budgets and make resource allocation decisions, few library and information organisations have adopted full-scale cost-analyses. Roberts suggests that this may in part be due to the fact that a library or information unit is typically part of a larger corporate organisation and thus for external purposes does not have to be subject to public financial accounting discipline. In any case as a cost-focus in a larger corporate body there is often little financial expertise available in the library or information unit itself.

It still seems that in many cases drawing up estimates and drafting a budget is likely to be the main financial and accounting task of many librarians and information managers. The literature also seems to confirm that despite well documented criticisms the familiar line by line budget remains the most commonly employed budgetary practice. Blagden (1982) and Kelly (1985) for example both provide useful discussions of the relative strength and weakness of a variety of budget formats. Certainly recent evidence suggests that the wave of interest in alternative budgeting processes such as PPBS (Planning-Programming Budgeting System) and ZBB (Zero Based Budgeting) does not seem to have been followed up by their widespread adoption in practice. As a result the main financial management decisions in libraries have tended to be concerned with maintaining existing provisions, or making only minor modifications to the cost of the service.

Cipfa Services (in the model developed for the Office of Arts and Libraries in 1987) identifies cost reduction and increased expectations about level and mix of services whilst Roberts (1982) stresses the inadequacies of line by line budgeting.

Part of these attempts to improve the level of cost data available to library managers has been the recent concern with the production of standardised costing procedures and the calculation of a range of unit costs for library services to allow for inter- as well as intra-library comparisons. The Cipfa report is one example of this process. However while such cost analysis is useful as an internal tool for monitoring costs and productivity, for indicating the cost of one service compared to another, and as a planning tool for budget preparation, the data provided does not in itself evaluate the quality of service provided. Perhaps the major theme therefore arising out of the recent literature on costing is the need to relate cost data to performance measures. Roberts (1982) himself comments that performance measures are incomplete if a cost and/or economic dimension cannot be included, and suggests that cost measurement is a necessary condition for the development of performance measures. This is not in itself a new concept as Bickman in 1971 for example strongly advocates the development of management information systems in which budgeting, accounting and performance measurement are fully integrated and mutually supporting. Indeed the authors of the Cipfa report admit that their own model costing system does not itself provide evaluation, but they claim that it will facilitate the inclusion of additional and more sophisticated measures of performance when these become available.

Another interesting costing concept is the one of marginal costing and as Robson (1988) makes clear the technique can be used in the evaluation of product mix decisions. As he states

"A change in product mix can be achieved by expanding or contracting sales or by substitution of one product for another. If sales are to be expanded within an existing set up there clearly has to be some spare capacity." Robson goes on "Marginal costing is based on an analysis of costs into those that are unaffected by

changes in the level of activity (fixed costs) and those that vary with changes in the level of activity. "

Two examples of how this principle has been applied to library situations can be found in Gold's (1975) attempt to devise an economic model for the allocation of an acquisitions budget, and Shohan's (1982) study which aims to infer the costs incurred because a library service is provided through a departmental library, rather than through a centralised library. Bickner (1971) in his study of the concepts of economic cost concludes that unless cost effectiveness ratios are equated at the margin, there is no way of ensuring the greatest effectiveness from the resources committed to any programme.

The relevance of this concept, and others drawn from economics, needs further investigation but with the pressures on libraries to develop new income generation services (ie products) a number of questions need to be asked.

i   Can marginal costing approaches be applied to a library that has a mix of free (at the point of consumption) and charged services?

ii   Is the assumption of spare capacity valid? For example a small increase in issues can be coped with in existing capacities but if the increase is significant then this must surely have an impact on capacity.

iii   If one assumes that library buildings and book stocks are fixed costs, increased utilisation through a new income generation service will nevertheless have an impact on service quality for the 'free' user.

iv   Should income generation services aim to recover all costs (or make a profit) including an equitable contribution to all overheads (buildings, stock, heating, lighting, etc) or should they simply attempt to recover the direct costs associated with the specific service?

One interesting postscript to this section on costing is that there appears to be little information on the costs of cost benefit studies. McElroy (1982) does however provide information on the costs of an extensive performance evaluation study he conducted.

17 PEER REVIEW

Costing techniques and inter library comparisons assess inputs to library and information systems. This is often the problem with peer reviews and accreditation.

The definition of accreditation as outlined by Estabrook (1987) in the proposal is a *"self regulatory process by which voluntary associations*

i   recognize institutions or programs that have been found to meet or exceed standards of quality, and

ii   assist in further improvement of the institutions or programs".

In this country the public libraries are a statutory service under the auspices of the Office of Arts and Libraries. Thus the Minister of Arts is empowered to institute an enquiry if a local authority is suspected of not providing a library service according to the terms of the 1964 Act. University libraries have for their part been generally included in the internal process of self-accreditation operated in the university sector.

It is rather the libraries of colleges and (after 1966) polytechnics which offer courses approved by the Council for National Academic Awards (CNAA) which have been subject to inspection as part of CNAA accreditation. The role of the CNAA is now of course changing with polytechnics having responsibility for self-accreditation as part of the move towards corporate status in 1989 and Davison (1988) maintains that the CNAA is now largely a spent force and will have little impact on library standards in the future.

The articles by Ashworth and Brewer (both 1984) for example discuss the impact that the CNAA has had on the development of libraries in polytechnics and colleges of higher education. Both, albeit with some reservations, conclude that on balance the influence of the CNAA has been a beneficial one, though Brewer especially doubts that there is much quantifiable evidence that colleges with CNAA validated courses have been better resourced than other institutions. Most importantly both acknowledge the difficulties confronting CNAA visits in accurately assessing the true quality of library services in terms of the time and measures available. This is perhaps reflected in the reluctance of the CNAA to apply standards. Indeed in 1971 the CNAA withdrew its standards issued two years previously because of fears that these would become used as 'maximum' standards and could in fact inhibit the development of higher quality services. The CNAA Libraries Panel consistently resisted pressure to reintroduce standards, according to Ashworth, because these would put too strong an emphasis on *"mere statistics of stock and accommodation"*, when the significant issues should be of a qualitative nature.

The experience of academic libraries in the United States which are subject to a regionally based accreditation process, seems to reveal a similar story. The articles by Charters (1985) and Bigelow (1985), both experienced members of regional accreditation teams, acknowledge the need for performance indicators that reveal how effectively library resources relate to educational programmes, and how library services are used by staff and students. Charter's comments that *"increasingly I am made aware through the evaluation of the process that adherence (or lack of adherence) to standards may not be the issue so much as is concern on the part of librarians about the use, or lack of utilisation, of college libraries"* is indicative of a growing realisation that accreditation based on standards relating to numbers of volumes, and issues of journals, etc, is of rather questionable value. Similarly Kania's (1988) study of the academic library standards of the seven regional accreditation commissions for higher education in the United States revealed that these differed by as much as 50% in length, style and content across the regions. She also concluded that the broad focus for library evaluation throughout the regions was still on inputs (collections, facilities, and staff) and processes (access and networking) rather than output measures.

It is perhaps heartening therefore that the proposal for a voluntary accreditation process for American public libraries (Estabrook 1987) lists, in addition to a number of more general goals, a number of objectives which specifically relate the process to evaluation. These include for example a commitment to *"require that the public library develops measurable objectives, consistent with the mission and goals, by which it may evaluate the effectiveness of its strategies"*, and *"verify that the mission, goals and objectives of the public library are subject to ongoing review and evaluation"*.

Estabrook admits that the fundamental problem raised by this is what happens if a library cannot achieve accreditation as a result of any number of reasons. Advocates of accreditation, such as Estabrook, however claim that this should not detract from the process because the element of self-study required has major benefits in that libraries will be forced to examine and review both their work and their role on a regular basis. Casserly (1987) in her review of self-study in academic libraries also suggests that this process by which an organisation analyses its goals, programmes, resources and effectiveness can induce change and lead to institutional development. Therefore whether accreditation is performed by the organisation itself or by an external body it is the self-study part of the process which the literature seems to suggest is the most valuable for the purposes of evaluation.

18 THE AMERICAN LIBRARY ASSOCIATION INITIATIVE

Dissatisfaction with existing national standards for public libraries (PLA 1966)* has also prompted the Public Library Association of the American Library Association to adopt a new approach which suggests that standards should be determined at local level and should be based on an analysis of the community a library serves, an examination of existing library services, and the decision of a planning committee regarding the goals and objectives of the library and its role in the local community. These principles were embodied in the PLA sponsored planning manual (Palmour et al 1980) which outlined recommendations for a continuous community based planning process in which libraries set goals and objectives based on identified needs and measured progress towards achieving these objectives. Information for this process was to be provided by a needs assessment of the local community using both printed secondary sources and primary data gathered from user surveys. The manual provided guidelines on the collection of input and output measures, but subsequent experience revealed inconsistencies in the data collection and analysis methods. See for example Bolt (1985) and Lynch (1983) for a discussion of the philosophy underlying this concern with the establishment of local standards for public libraries.

The need to provide a more consistent approach to data collection was recognized in the PLA manual on output measures (Zweizig and Rodger 1982). The manual describes twelve output measures selected on the basis of their relevance to commonly occurring public library goals and relative ease of collection. They include six per capita measures, ie circulation, in-library materials use, library visits, programme attendance, reference transactions, and registration, three materials availability measures, ie title fill rate, subject and author fill rate, and browser fill rate, as well as turnover rate, reference fill rate, and document delivery.

Since its publication the manual has been the subject of considerable debate regarding the utility of the measures described. Goldhor (1983) for example was quick to raise fears concerning the somewhat simplistic approach adopted, and the emphasis placed by the measures on **quantitative** rather than qualitative valuations of library output. More importantly perhaps Goldhor, and D'Elia (1985), D'Elia and Walsh (1985) and most recently D'Elia and Rodger (1987) have cast doubts on the validity of the measures claiming that they are prone to statistical error and affected by differences in user experience and behaviour. D'Elia's work in particular has been concerned with the hypothesis that libraries that differed in the quantity of resources available would differ in their ability to meet the needs of their users, and that these differences in performance would be reflected in the behaviour of the patrons using the libraries. However in his surveys D'Elia has found no meaningful relationship between patrons' uses of the library and either their reasons for selecting the library or their evaluation of the library's facilities. He concludes therefore that output measures affected by

---

*   Public Library Association Standards Committee, minimum standards for
      public library systems (1966) Chicago, American Library Association.

user behaviour are of questionable value to the assessment of library performance.

Advocates of the PLA manual have acknowledged some of the limitations inherent in their output measures and have made suggestions for future improvement and refinements to the techniques. For example McClure et al (1986) recognize the margin of statistical error in many of the output measures but claim that more sophisticated statistical analysis ignores the primary objectives of the manual in that there must be a trade-off between the quality of the measures, the data they produce, and the ability of users to understand such measures. They claim that critics have overlooked the management context for the utility of the measures, in that they are above all intended as internal indicators of library performance rather than measures for comparisons between libraries, or used in isolation for making definitive judgements on a service. Zweizig (1987) reiterated this point in saying that evaluation should be seen not as a process leading to a judgement, *"is it good or is it bad"*, but as a means of *"providing information that helps us do better"*. He sums up the primary value of output measures as *"doing quick things that will help us manage better"*. This philosophy was underlined in the revised editions of both manuals which appeared in 1987 (McClure et al 1987, and Van House et al 1987).

The evidence derived from literature of practical attempts to implement the PLA's output measures is somewhat mixed. For example Owen (1985) and Baker (1987) both suggest that there is comparatively little use of the PLA's recommendations on planning and output measures amongst the US state public library systems. However a number of other reports serve to demonstrate both the inherent limitations and potential benefits of using these types of output measures. Seff (1987) reports that attempts to use output measures as funadamental indicators of success in reaching selected objectives appeared fruitless when projected increases fell within the margin of error for the library's sample size. Nevertheless she comments that the **process** of analysing the measures has been more useful than the **statistics** themselves. Seff cites the following examples, including the analysis of patron requests, which enabled the library to make the acquisition of duplicate copies more responsive to user demand, and which possibly contributed to an overall increase in circulation; document delivery figures suggested improvements to reserve procedures; and the high referred rate in a reference fill survey indicated possible training priorities to improve reference services.

Similarly the report by Manthey and Brown (1985) not only provides an interesting account of an attempt to apply output measures to a special library, in this case a hospital library, but it also demonstrates very clearly the need for additional, more qualitative, indicators of performance. Here again the output measures seem to raise more questions than they answer. For example circulation per capita did nothing to explain the value of the collection to the various segments of the client community; reference transactions per capita did not explain why one group of users asked fewer reference questions than others; and reference fill rate showed the percentage of reference questions answered promptly but did not provide any clue as to the accuracy or value of the answers given. The authors again concluded that the questions raised as a result of the measurement process proved to be more valuable than the actual figures produced.

The two examples above do seem to support the view that the output measures which are relatively quick and inexpensive to collect can assist and encourage library managers to adopt some performance monitoring process. Caution however must be exercised in the interpretation of what the figures actually reveal about the library services examined, and demonstrate the need for the application of more in depth 'qualitative' evaluation studies to perhaps provide answers to the questions raised by the analysis.

19 METHODOLOGY

It is important too when undertaking any evaluative study to ensure that it is based on a sound methodology. Line and Stone (1982) provide an excellent starting point for gaining an understanding of the strengths and weaknesses of the wide range of techniques that are available. Again, just as there is no one single criterion for assessing performance so there is not one methodological technique that can be deployed.

Invariably most evaluative studies will involve questioning the user and non user. It is essential therefore that such techniques as interviews and questionnaires are designed and pilot tested with maximum care. Again the Line and Stone (1982) monograph is strongly recommended as is the paper by Bookstein (1985) which reviews in a library setting many of the common faults made in questionnaire design.

All commentators emphasise that a wide range of techniques should be deployed and good examples of this are the investigations conducted by Allen (1984), Brember and Leggate (1985), King Research (1982) and McElroy (1982). Some innovative techniques used include solution development records (Allen); conjoint measurement (Ramsing and Wish 1982, and Griffiths and King 1986); budget gaming (McElroy); telephone surveys (King Research); communication networks (Allen); expected value of perfect information (Wills and Christopher 1970); derived value (Oldman 1978); Likert technique (Totterdell and Bird 1978).

Brember and Leggate (1985) by utilising a number of different techniques produce what they describe as a 'rich picture' of the library services that they were investigating. This rich picture is so necessary for studies concerned with evaluating the system as a whole and Goodall (1988) rightly points out that most evaluative investigations tend to concentrate on only one part of a service.

Chelton (1987) rightly emphasises the importance of being clear about the objectives of evaluation, ie what is it you are trying to assess. In the context of services for children, Chelton demonstrates how two different aims of children's services (the stimulation of reading and the improvement of reading skills) can be assessed. Commentators emphasise the need for replicated studies to validate results, the importance of control groups and the need for 'before and after' studies.

Suchman (1967) in an earlier but still relevant monograph lucidly explains why control groups are necessary. Suchman also suggests a three step process in assessing the validity of a selected criterion:-

i   Is the criterion selected a valid criterion of what is to be measured (eg is improved job performance a valid criterion for therapeutic gains)?

ii   Is the indicator selected a valid reflection of the gains (eg is increased production a valid criterion of improved job performance)?

iii   Are the various valid segments of the study combined in such a way as to preserve their individual validity and achieve validity as a whole?

One final point on methodology is that the most refined and reliable techniques can fail if the investigation lacks the support of the staff in the library being evaluated. The difficulties of gaining this support should not be underestimated as the survey of librarians' attitudes to evaluation by Bird (1981) makes clear.

20 CASE HISTORIES OR THE EXPANDED ANECDOTE

Blagden (1980) summarised a number of spectacular technological disasters which could perhaps have been avoided if the technologist had access to information that had already been published prior to the disaster. Of course this assumes that libraries would have been able to retrieve the information at the time it was wanted and that the overall costs of library investment did not outweigh these potential savings.

Clearly all library and information services can benefit from the recording of one off success stories, as Wilde and Cooper report (1988), where access to information significantly increased the profits or significantly reduced the costs of the organisation that the service is supporting. These case histories do not answer the question referred to earlier as to whether, in **general** terms, the benefits from the library service outweigh the costs unless the library can demonstrate large one off cost reductions or profit improvements. In the absence of such dramatic evidence one has to turn to the more representative evidence which will be gathered using reliable methodology which was referred to in the previous section.

21 DOCUMENT DELIVERY AND AVAILABILITY

An area which has developed a sound methodology which will give generalised representative results, is the area of document delivery and availability. High methodological standards were set by Orr and others as far back as 1968 when they developed a methodology for assessing a library's ability to deliver known documents.

The technique has been extensively used and reviews of its strengths and weaknesses have been presented by Lancaster (1977). It should be emphasised that the technique is only assessing document supply success rates and speed of delivery.

Revill (1987) reviews availability rates, ie on the shelf when sought, and quotes availability rates from other studies of 60%, 70%, 50-60% and 56%. Revill admits however that given the development of online public access catalogues these studies may be less useful in the future. This is because users will be able to check whether an item is on loan and may not so frequently in future go directly to the shelves without checking the catalogue.

Buckland (1975) was one of the first to conduct availability studies where he assessed satisfaction levels against 'objective' availability measures. He found that if one improves the availability of material one also improves satisfaction. However this improved availability increases users expectation which over a longer period **reduces** satisfaction levels if availability fails to improve in the longer term.

22 INCREASED RESOURCES

The problem of trying to cope with users' increased expectation with declining budgets may well make some despair of the whole evaluative process. Assessing expectation and attitudes towards the library is only one approach and of course with unlimited resources one could simply ensure that the library had every book required immediately available: the user's definition of the perfect library.

Unlimited resources are not an option but, as Orr (1968) suggests, increases in resources will (other things being equal) tend to improve service quality, but not necessarily proportionally. It is that word proportionally that is the key to the funders' dilemma: what improved benefits do we get from an increase in library investment? Techniques such as zero based budgeting and sensitivity analyses can help shed light on these questions. Chelton (1987) however comments (in the context of children's libraries) that researchers found that putting standard resources into a library did not necessarily produce standard intermediate output measures, eg issues per head.

23 ATTITUDES TOWARDS PERFORMANCE ASSESSMENT

Most library managers perceive that one of the key indicators of their degree of success or failure is their ability to increase their budget either in real terms and/or in comparison with other similar library and information services. There is clearly no certainty that, if you have a well managed library which is regularly and systematically evaluated, that process will lead automatically to an improved level of resourcing. However the trend in all organisations seems to be clear; justify your existence otherwise adequate resourcing will be difficult to obtain.

Bird (1981) in a survey of attitudes of libraries towards performance assessment discovered that there was strong agreement about the need, but considerable doubt as to whether the means were available to implement credible performance assessment studies. Brockman (1984) similarly found a strong desire for more research in the area of cost benefit and output studies although new technology was perceived to have an even higher priority. It should be noted that these two areas of course are not mutually exclusive.

McClure (1986) in a survey of US academic librarians' attitudes toward performance assessment concluded that

i   there was little faith in cost data and performance measures

ii   that such information rarely has much impact on decision making

iii   that in-house data frequently lacks validity and reliability, and

iv   that libraries are too understaffed to take time away from the provision of services to identify, collect and analyse such data

Bird (1981) also discovered that concern over the cost of these studies was another barrier to undertaking performance evaluation.

24 CONCLUSION

On the basis of this review and previous experience there is undoubtedly a wide range of credible, low-cost approaches to performance evaluation. However use of these approaches is not very widespread and there is a significant lack of replication so that one cannot make judgements on how reliable these approaches really are.

The focus of library evaluation should still in our view be to show the part that libraries **and** librarians play in enriching the minds of women and men.

This then was the theme of the work by Blagden (1980) and Goodall (1988) found it surprising that *"even in 1980 Blagden felt that he had to emphasise that library performance measures must increasingly be based on outputs"*. In the conclusion to her 1988 articles Goodall maintains that future efforts at measurement must concentrate on output. **Plus ca change**.

In the end one has to change attitudes radically. Librarians pay lip service to the need for more effective performance evaluation but for all sorts of understandable reasons do little or nothing about performance evaluation in practice. New technology will help as better management information systems emerge. In addition it is suggested that more effective dissemination of this knowledge will also speed up the take up of performance evaluation, possibly on the lines suggested in the multi media publishing project which is currently under active consideration by the British Library.

25 ACKNOWLEDGEMENTS

Our thanks to the support of the British Library R & D Department in general and Brian Perry and Maureen Grieves in particular, and to Dr D Lewis of Aslib who first floated the idea. Our thanks also to Geoff Smith of Leicester Public Libraries, Lynne Brindley of the University of Aston, and Dr Sandra Ward of Glaxo who have agreed to assess the review and explore the possibilities of further publishing initiatives.

Last and by no means least our thanks to Sally Eilbeck for typing the report and progress chasing it to a successful conclusion.

ANNOTATED BIBLIOGRAPHY

Allen, Thomas J. Managing the flow of technology: technology transfer and the dissemination of technological information within the R & D organisation. (1984) Paperback edition, Cambridge, Mass, MIT Press, 320p.

This is a revised edition of a book which when it first appeared in 1977 set out to summarise more than a decade of work on communications flow in science and engineering organisations. The book discusses for example how technological information is acquired by an R & D organisation, demonstrates the importance of technical communication in the R & D process, and originates the idea of the 'gate keeper' in the information transfer process. The chapters on the evaluation of communication networks discuss a number of useful methodological approaches. Allen concludes by making a number of recommendations for improving the communications within an organisation.

Allred, John. The measurement of library services: an appraisal of current problems and possibilities. (1979) Library Management vol.1(2), p.2-46.

Author argues that it is a mistake to assume that we are simply looking for clever measures with which to allow us to make links between the desired outcomes and the best methods with which to achieve these outcomes. He accepts that output measurement is an improvement but not the answer, refreshing as it is to judge a library by the quantity of what comes out rather than what is put in. The author believes that the nature of the library service is that of a 'broad aim' social programme best judged (evaluated) by gathering politically significant information on the consequences of political acts.

Aren, Lisa J; Webreck, Susan J; Patrick, Mark. Costing library operations - a bibliography. (1987) Collection Building vol.8(3), p.23-28.

Compiled as part of a University of Michigan library project to calculate staff time spent on library tasks and the costs associated with staff and services, this bibliography focuses particularly on the literature of data collection techniques. It does provide annotations for the sources judged to be of particular value.

Armstrong, Charles M. Measurement and evaluation of the public library. (1968) Chapter 2, in Research methods in librarianship: measurement and evaluation, edited by Herbert Goldhor, Champaign, Illinois, University of Illinois, 131p.

Armstrong's paper begins with a brief discussion of the theory of evaluation. According to Armstrong the ultimate point of measurement and evaluation is its product - "Does it produce what it is designed to produce, and does it meet the requirements of the customers?" He suggests therefore that the ultimate product of the library is intangible. (Compare this approach to that of Lancaster (1977).) The rest of Armstrong's paper is concerned with the measurement of various library facilities and processes, and he emphasises the need to review these in the context of the desired ultimate product.

Ashworth, Wilfred. Library development: the polytechnics. (1984) Library Review vol.33 (Autumn), p.132-138.

Contribution to a review of the impact of the Council for National Academic Awards on the development of libraries in polytechnics and colleges of higher education. Suggests that the CNAA was one of a number of factors behind a steady improvement in book stock, staff provision and accommodation, and regards the influence of the CNAA on polytechnic libraries as having been generally beneficial.

Audit Commission. Performance review in local government. (1986) HMSO.

This document raises some interesting questions such as are public libraries motivated by any of its attempts at performance measurement, and what do librarians regard as success given a background of poor accountability, absence of direct pricing and low public interest and expectation. This report does not provide the answers to these questions and the implication is that these questions will need to be resolved within the profession.

Ayris, P. The stimulation of creativity: a review of the literature concerning the concept of browsing 1970-85. (1986) CRUS Working Paper No.5, Sheffield, University of Sheffield, Consultancy and Research Unit, 112p.

Ayris points out that although browsing plays an important part in the selection of books in public libraries, it is often claimed that the value of browsing is unsupported by verifiable data. Ayris however describes two methodologies to measure browsing activities in public and academic libraries. His findings indicate that browsing is in fact practised by patrons in libraries of both types.

Bailey, Bill. The "55 percent rule" revisited. Contribution to The Continuing Debate on Library Reference Service: a Mini-Symposium. (1987) Journal of Academic Librarianship vol.13(5), p.280-281.

This article is a contribution to the debate on the validity of unobtrusive testing inspired particularly by the work of advocates of the technique, Hernon and McClure (1987). As with the contribution by Schumacher (1987) this article represents the views of a practising reference librarian.

Baker, Sharon L. Exploring the use of output measures for public libraries in North Carolina public libraries. (1987) New York, US Department of Education. Educational Resources Information Center Report.

The study was designed to determine the extent of the application of the recommendations described in the manuals, A planning process for public libraries (Palmour, V.E. et al 1980) and Output measures for public libraries (Zweizig and Rodgers 1982), in North Carolina's public libraries. The author concludes that the state library system appears to be following a national pattern of non-use of the two manuals.

Beckman, M. The importance of measuring library effectiveness. (1987) Bibliotecha Medica Canadiana vol.8(4), p.180-189.

The author maintains that library performance can be assessed using the following criteria: availability, accessibility, reliability, relevance, timeliness, portability, and how conducive the overall library environment is to effective information utilisation. The future impact of new technology is stressed especially such developments as compact discs, microcomputers and distributed processing, all of which can lead to the library being bypassed.

Bickner, Robert E. Concepts of economic cost, in Cost consideration in systems analysis. (1971) edited by Gene H Fisher, New York. American Elsevier, p.24-63. Reprinted in, Key papers in the economics of information, edited by Donald W King, Nancy K Roderer, Harold A Olsen, White Plains, New York, Knowledge Industry Publications, 1983, 327p.

This article presents a discussion of a number of theoretical aspects of cost, especially the concept or measurement of cost in terms of benefits lost. Among the other issues included are cost versus benefits, the identification, measurement and evaluation of costs, past and future costs, minimising costs/maximising benefits, and macro versus micro cost analysis. It should be noted that the examples used to illustrate these points are not directly related to information science but explore concepts which are transferable.

Bigelow, Linda. Indicators of need, costs and quality in LRC program evaluation. (1985) Community & Junior College Libraries vol.4(1), p.43-48.

Written by an experienced accreditation team member, this article discusses the need to include input and output measures in the review process in order to facilitate assessments regarding the quality and relevance of library and learning resources services.

Birbeck, Vaughan P; Whittaker, Kenneth A. Room for improvement: an unobtrusive testing of British public library reference service. (1987) Public Library Journal vol.2(4), p.55-60.

Interesting example of a recent attempt to apply the technique of unobtrusive testing to a British library situation.

Bird, Jean. Assessing effectiveness: a preliminary study of the views of public librarians September 1979-May 1980. (1981) Polytechnic of North London. British R & D Report 5632.

Interviews, group discussions, checklists and questionnaires were employed with different levels of staff in ten authorities to assess the views of librarians towards performance evaluation. There was general agreement about the need for performance evaluation but considerable concern was expressed as to whether it could be done effectively and concern was also expressed that the costs of attempting evaluation exercises might be prohibitive. Respondents all stressed the importance of ensuring that library staff were supportive of any exercises that might be conducted.

Blagden, J. Some thoughts on use and users. (1988) Iatul Quarterly vol.2(3), p.125-134.

Examines the concept of use in the context of performance measurement. Specifically comments on the methodological problems associated with assessing use in general as well as looking at how well a particular service is reaching a specific user group. The issue of what relationship use has to the corporate goals that the library is seeking to support is also explored.

Blagden, J. Financial Management, in Handbook of Special Librarianship, by Wilfred Ashworth. (1982) 5th rev.ed. by L J Anthony, London: Aslib.

The author attempts to highlight some key financial issues affecting libraries, and makes a number of practical suggestions as to how these might be tackled. He also outlines the strengths and weaknesses of different ways of capturing and recording financial information. Among the techniques discussed are line-by-line, performance budgets and zero based budgets. The author also indicates the importance of relating costs to the performance of individual services and describes methods of justifying investments in library and information services. Finally the author discusses some of the implications of charging for library services.

Blagden, J. Do we really need libraries? (1980) Clive Bingley.

Reviews the literature emphasising the importance of outputs, outcomes and how effective libraries are in supporting corporate goals. Introduces the techniques of market penetration: how well a library service is getting through to its customers; and impact: what effect the service has on those that are exposed to its outputs.

Blagden, J. Special libraries. (1975) Library Association Record vol.77(6), p.129-133.

In a discussion of library effectiveness the author describes the results of a somewhat restricted study designed to ascertain the costs of obtaining information from external sources in a 'libraryless' situation compared with acquiring that same information through an in house library. According to the author, this study does show both the time savings and superior quality of answers provided by an in house library. However, he does admit that this assumes all the information supplied was useful and the small size of the sample on which the study was based could undermine the validity of the results.

Bolt, Nancy. Performance measures for public libraries in, Public libraries and the challenges of the next two decades. (1985) edited by Alphonse F Trezza, Littleton, Colorado, Libraries Unlimited, p.47-55.

Provides a useful summary of the development of performance measures for public libraries in the United States, from the publication of the Minimum Standards in 1966 to the PLA sponsored manuals of the 1980s. (See Palmour, Vernon E. 1980 and Zweizig and Roderer 1982.)

Bookstein, A. Questionnaire research in a library setting. (March 1985) Journal of Academic Librarianship vol.11(1), p.24-33.

The author argues that the questionnaire as a device for obtaining information is very seriously flawed. This article reports data from two experiments which attempt to show the degree to which people differ in their interpretation of questions referring to library services and the implications of this when interpreting survey results.

Brember, V L. Linking a medical user survey to management for library effectiveness, II - a Checkland soft systems study. (June 1985) Journal of Documentation vol.41(2), p.59-74.

The soft systems methodology developed by Checkland was chosen as a way of relating the evidence of a user survey to the practical problems of library management.

Brember, V L; Leggate, P. Linking a medical user survey to management for library effectiveness, I - the user survey. (March 1985) Journal of Documentation vol.41(1), p.1-14.

This paper reports an intensive survey of medical library users in the Oxford teaching hospitals and university science departments. The study employed a multiple methodologic approach including questionnaires, interviews, direct observation, analysis of records and simple feedback forms. This approach enabled the researchers to produce a rich picture of the users and their interaction with the library service.

Brewer, Gordon. Library development: the colleges and institutes of higher education. (1984) vol.33 Autumn, p.139-152.

Outlines the role of the CNAA in the development of libraries in colleges and institutes of higher education. Reports the views of college librarians that on balance the CNAA has been helpful although Brewer suggests there is little quantitative evidence to support a conclusion that colleges with CNAA validated courses have been better resourced than other institutions.

Brockman, J R. Academic library management research: an evaluative review. (1984) Centre for Library and Information Management, Loughborough University.

The author presents a critical review of published research into the effectiveness of academic library management. He also reports the results of a survey of UK academic libraries the object of which was to identify key management problems. By comparing published research with the survey findings a number of research gaps were identified including new technology, managerial attitudes, staff mobility and assessments of the future.

Brookes, Bertram C. The estimation of populations engaged in intermittent activities in information contexts. (1979) International Forum on Information and Documentation vol.4(2), p.12-18.

This article discusses the problem of estimating a total population from its observed activities. Brookes uses data from a number of information activities to examine whether or not it is valid to regard recorded use over a short time scale as true random samples on which to base predictions of future usage.

Buckland, M K. Concepts of library goodness. (April 1982) Canadian Library Journal vol.39(2), p.63-66.

A brief review of differing perceptions of library goodness largely based on the earlier work by Orr. The author emphasises that there cannot be a single measure of library goodness.

Buckland, M K. Book availability and the library user. (1975) New York, Pergamon Press Inc, 196p.

In this book Buckland provides both a theoretical as well as a practical study of stock control. The emphasis of the author's approach is to relate acquisition, duplication, binding, circulation and discarding to the needs and behaviour of library users. Among the topics discussed are stock size and retention periods, and the impact of binding policies and borrowing on availability. This latter area is examined in some detail, and reference is made to a case study at the University of Lancaster which attempts to demonstrate for example the relationship between availability and satisfaction levels in measures of library performance.

Cabinet Office, Information Technology Advisory Panel. Making a business of information - a survey of new opportunities. (1983) London, HMSO, 53p.

This report provides a summary of developments in Information Technology and the implications of these for those involved in the supply of information. The authors of the report identify an expanding 'tradeable information sector' and attempt to show how government and the private sector could both encourage the further exploitation of IT in order to enhance overseas earnings.

Carley, Michael. Performance monitoring in a professional public service - the case of the careers service. (1988) PSI research report 685, London, Policy Studies Institute, 157p.

This case study begins by examining recent progress in outcome measurement under the government's Financial Management Initiative which has affected many aspects of administration in central government departments. Carley then explores the potential for a simple and cost efficient monitoring programme for the Careers Service. This provides a useful model, aspects of which could be applicable in other professional services including libraries and information. In particular, Carley's discussion of the problems of client satisfaction suggest that clients can be dissatisfied with a perfectly adequate service because of a variety of unmet needs which the service is not designed to meet.

Carter, M P. A methodology for the economic appraisal of management information. (December 1986) International Journal of Information Management vol.6(4), p.193-201.

An approach to the economic appraisal of management information is outlined. Four stages in this process are outlined (i) assessing managers' information needs (ii) putting a value on the information identified in stage one (iii) the cost of that information (iv) the cost benefit analyses arising out of stages (i) and (ii). A useful list of common pitfalls to be avoided is included in the paper.

Casserly, Mary F. Accreditation related self-study as a planned change process - factors relating to its success in academic libraries. (1987) Journal of Library Administration vol.8(1), p.85-105.

Emphasises the value of self-study in the accreditation process and describes the results of a survey designed to identify the factors which seem to determine the success of self-study. Casserly recommends emphasis on the approach and planning factors, ie internal motivation, commitment, leadership and design, for successful self-study.

Centre for Interfirm Comparison. Inter-library comparisons. (1981) British Library Research and Development Report No.5638, British Library Board.

This report gives the results of an inter-library comparison, conducted on a pilot basis with library systems drawn from various types of public authorities throughout Great Britain. It sets out the objectives of such comparisons, the principles underlying its design, outlines the methods used, and provides tables of results. The report also makes recommendations for further development of the technique. It represents an attempt to provide libraries with information on how resources are being applied to various functions, and to calculate unit costs for each activity. The authors of the report concede that measures representing the value, utility or benefit of these activities are not used because they were not generally available. On its own therefore the cost data contained in this report does not reveal anything about the relative quality of the services offered, and thus the technique may be of limited value to the more general question of performance measurement.

Charters, Margaret L. To use standards, or not to use standards - is that the question? (1985) Community & Junior College Libraries vol.4(1) p.39-42.

Describes the limitations of existing standards for regional accreditation and emphasises the need to introduce new criteria for measuring the quality and effectiveness of college libraries in the United States.

Chelton, M K. Evaluation of children's services. (Winter 1987) Library Trends vol.35(3), p.463-484.

A discussion of programme evaluation concepts and methods is presented in which specific attention is given to the ways these concepts and methods can be applied to children's libraries. Approaches to the assessment of programmes concerned with the stimulation of reading and the improvement of reading skills are outlined. It is emphasised that evaluation will only work where there is support for evaluative research and a willingness to act on its findings.

Childers, Thomas. The quality of reference: still moot after 20 years. Contribution to, Library Reference Service: an Unrecognised Crisis - a Symposium. (1987) Journal of Academic Librarianship vol.13(2), p.73-74.

This article questions particularly whether results from unobtrusive tests can be used to make generalisations about the reference process as a whole. Childers emphasises the need to relate all the various aspects of the reference service to the philosophies, objectives, policies and demographics of individual libraries to arrive at an informed perspective on the quality of the reference service.

Clark, P M. New approaches to the measurement of public library use by individual patrons. (1983) Graduate School of Library and Information Science, University of Illinois. Occasional Paper No.162.

Based upon the concept that library use measurement should have as its basic starting point the individual user, the paper provides a method by which it can be determined who borrows and how much over a period of time. This technique can produce more accurate global market penetration data and can divide users into heavy and light usage. Typically the application of the technique shows that a small proportion of borrowers (5%) can account for 30% of all borrowing transactions.

Clarke, M; Stewart, I. Local government and the public service orientation. (1985) Luton, Local Government Training Board.

In this discussion of local government services, the authors argue that even if authorities are concerned to provide what they think their customers need, they must first address the question of what their customers want. They stress that any authority which fails to do this is not providing a service for the customer but is merely offering that service to the customer.

Cronin, B. Taking the measure of service. (June/July 1982) Aslib Proceedings vol.34(6/7), p.273-294.

Describes techniques for evaluating the effectiveness of public library services in which he stresses the importance of evaluation against specific meaningful objectives. Techniques reviewed include unobtrusive testing, approaches to stock management, document delivery, evaluation of current awareness services, and attitude measurements.

Cronin, B. Performance measurement and information management. (May 1982) Aslib Proceedings vol.34(5), p.227-236.

The author outlines approaches to performance evaluation including document delivery tests, failure analyses, and unobtrusive testing. A report is also given of the results of interviews with library and information managers on their attitudes towards evaluation. A checklist was used in these interviews which included specific evaluative criteria for current awareness and information retrieval services and approaches to document delivery assessment.

Crowley, Terence. Half-right reference: is it true? (1985) RQ vol.25(1), p.59-68.

This article reviews a number of the major studies of unobtrusive reference tests including the methodology used and the results obtained.

Davison, Donald. Academic libraries in the enterprise culture. (1988) Library Association.

The author maintains that the restructured funding of universities and polytechnics will encourage a more entrepreneurial approach to the management of academic institutions. It will provide possibly greater opportunities for income generating activities but these activities will pose a potential threat to library services whose costs are often not directly recoverable from the user.

The author reviews these problems, suggests some solutions and argues for a more active role by the Library Association in this area.

D'Elia, George D. Materials availability fill rates - useful measures of library performance. (1985) Public Libraries vol.24(3), p.106-110.

This paper examines the validity of using three measures of materials availability, i.e. title fill rate, subject and author fill rate and browsers fill rate, as proposed by the PLA sponsored Output measures for public libraries (Zweizig and Rodger 1982) with reference to libraries in the Saint Paul Public Library system. D'Elia concludes that none of the user success rates and none of the fill rates calculated from the data obtained from the surveys could be used to compare libraries of the SPPL system or to assist in resource allocation decisions. He concludes that the materials availability rates were error bound, i.e. there is unexplained 'variance' or 'imprecision' in the figures, and were not useful indicators of library performance. D'Elia also suggests that availability measures may be actually measuring user success in, or skills for, obtaining library materials.

D'Elia, George D; Rodger, E J. Comparative assessment of patron uses and evaluation across public libraries within a system: a replication. (Jan-Mar 1987) Library and Information Science Research vol.9(1), p.5-20.

In house surveys of patrons were conducted in each of the twenty libraries of a county public library system. While the libraries differed in the amount of resources made available to patrons the analyses of survey data indicated that (i) there were no meaningful differences among the samples in the reasons given for selecting the library to visit (ii) there were no meaningful differences among the samples in their uses of the library (iii) there were meaningful differences among the samples in their evaluations of the facilities of the library visited (iv) there were no meaningful relationships between the patrons' uses of the library and either their reasons for selecting the library or their evaluations of the library's facilities. It is claimed that these results corroborate earlier findings and provide additional evidence as to the idiosyncratic nature of patron behaviour.

D'Elia, George D; Walsh, Sandra. Patrons' uses and evaluations of library services: a comparison across five public libraries. (1985) Library & Information Science Research, vol.7(1), p.3-30.

This paper reports on a study designed to test the hypothesis that differences in library performance will be reflected in client use of the library. The authors concluded that different levels of resources and different levels of performance had no discernible effect upon patrons' uses and evaluations of those libraries. The conclusions drawn from this study had to be tempered somewhat by a concern that qualitative differences among the libraries could have minimised due to centralisation of policy and acquisitions because the libraries were all part of the same Ramsey County public library system.

Deloitte, Haskins and Sells Associates. An evaluation of Alberta's education library service. (1986) ED0274363.

This evaluation was largely based on interviewing users and library staff. On site observation of libraries and a review of library records were also included in the investigation. The study concluded that the objectives of the library service were unclear and that some organisational changes would overcome some of the problems identified.

Dervin, B; Clarke M. ASQ: Asking significant questions. Alternative tools for information need and accountability assessments for libraries. (1987) Belmont, Peninsular Library System for California State Library.

This manual is designed to present librarians in the State of California with an alternative 'sense making' approach to assessing the needs of customers and potential customers and to assess how effectively the libraries are in meeting those needs. The manual includes interesting examples of the types of questions to be asked, all of which are based on a triangle of situation - gaps - help. Answers to these questions can be used to develop a typology of needs as well as assessing the effectiveness of the service.

Dumont, R R. A conceptual basis for library effectiveness. (March 1980) College and Research Libraries vol.41(2), p.103-111.

Author argues that there are many definitions of library effectiveness and claims that a new model based on systems theory may minimise the difficulties of trying to deploy a number of effectiveness criteria at the same time.

Durrance, J C. Knowing the cost of everything and the value of nothing. (1987) Collection Building vol.8(1), p.35-36.

The author maintains that the library profession must be cautious about accepting economic concepts developed and grounded on private enterprise principles. She advocates examining economic principles dispassionately in conjunction with the tenets espoused by the profession and only applied after their compatability is established.

Dyer, E R; O'Connor, D O. A Proposed methodology to evaluate school libraries. (Winter 1983) Journal of Educational Media and Library Sciences vol.20(2), p.119-135. *

The authors review the history of evaluation in US school libraries. The authors point out that the late 1960s and early 1970s were very much the eras of the checklist which reached its pinnacle with the Purdue Self Evaluation System consisting of over 274 check points (Loertscher D V, Stroud J G. The Purdue Self Evaluation System School Media Centers. (1976) Hi Willow Research & Publishing). The authors also provide a critique of various approaches to ranking libraries by scores and they suggest using a library quotient calculation which assumes a standard deviation of 15 from say an arbitrary norm of 100. Libraries scoring less than 85 or more than 115 will be deemed to have significantly better or poorer performance than libraries scoring between 85 and 115.

*   Paper was originally published in Information and Library Manager (December 1983) vol.2(3).

Emery, C D. Library patrons as consumers: the application of the theory of repeat buying to the investigation of library use patterns. (1987) Cranfield Institute of Technology, Department of Social Policy, MPhil thesis. 279p.

According to Emery research into library use has failed to address the fundamental behavioural dimension of the problem. The author believes that marketing and consumer studies can provide a reservoir of relevant substantive theory. He describes the results of field work at Cranfield Institute of Technology and the University of Waterloo which show that segments of user populations exhibit distinctive use patterns, both with respect to the amount of use and the types and subject content of the material borrowed. In particular Emery argues that the Negative Binomial Distribution, which models repeat buying patterns, is applicable to the observed repeat use patterns of library patrons, and suggests that the NBD model could provide a mechanism for incorporating marketing concepts such as product mix and brand switching into the study of library use.

Estabrook, Leigh. Accreditation of public libraries: an outrageous suggestion? (1987) Library Journal vol.112(15), p.35-38.

Outlines proposals for voluntary accreditation process for public libraries in the United States. Discusses the problems involved and the likely benefits of accreditation, and stresses the importance of ongoing review and evaluation.

Evans, P A et al. An instrument for measuring the effectiveness of information systems. (1988) Computers and Industrial Engineering vol.12(3), p.277-236.

Sophisticated questionnaires and analysis techniques were used to determine needs, utility of information, information flows and user satisfaction. Statistical approaches to the analysis of responses are also given. One technique involved almost seven hours of interview time per respondent but some of the questionnaires could be useful in an abbreviated form for studies of information need in a library context.

Fischhoff, B. Cost benefit analysis and the art of motorcycle maintenance. (1977) Policy Sciences vol.8, p.177-202.

This paper critically evaluates the technique of cost benefit analysis. Specifically the author discusses cost benefit analyses in terms of their rationale, acceptability, problems, misuse, and how such analyses might be improved. It should be noted here that cost benefit analysis is primarily perceived as a means of assessing whether a particular project should proceed or not. Clearly it is rare for library investment decisions to be assessed on this basis and such investments are more normally assessed on what levels of library investment might apply. Nevertheless the methodology outlined in this paper has some relevance to library and information evaluation.

Flowerdew, A D J; Whitehead, C M E. Cost effectiveness and cost/benefit analysis in information science. (1974) OSTI Report 5206, London, London School of Economics and Political Science. 71p.

Flowerdew and Whitehead provide a critical survey of studies of costs, effectiveness and benefit measures in the field of scientific and technical information. They begin with a series of definitions and then list the kinds of problems for which cost effectiveness and cost benefit analysis can be used. They also suggest an economic framework to illustrate the ways in which information differs from other goods and services. They conclude for example that the price a user is willing to pay for information may not in fact be a measure of the full benefit to the purchaser. The report concludes with recommendations for further research.

Gers, Ralph; Seward, Lille J. Improving reference performance - results of a statewide study. (1985) Library Journal, November 1, p.32-35.

One of the largest-scale unobtrusive tests yet attempted, the results of which are similar to those achieved in other surveys in that 55% of questions were answered correctly.

Goldhor, Herbert. [Review] Output measures for public libraries: a manual of standardized procedures by Douglas Zweizig and Eleanor Jo Rodger, Chicago, American Library Association. (1982) The Library Quarterly, vol.33(2), p.180-181.

This review applauds the attempt to place the emphasis for evaluating library services on output measures rather than traditional counts of input variables. However the reviewer does raise a number of reservations which include: a number of the proposed measures will be affected by differences in user behaviour and experience; at least half the measures are concerned purely with quantitative rather than qualitative indicators; and some of the techniques suggested are perhaps too simplistic.

Goodall, D L. Performance measurement: a historical perspective. (1988) Journal of Librarianship vol.20(2), p.128-144.

A primarily descriptive review of literature from 1966 to date.

Gold, Stephen D. Allocating the book budget: an economic model. (1975) College and Research Libraries vol.36(5), p.397-402.

In his attempt to devise an economic model for the allocation of a book budget, Gold explores the concept of both marginal cost and marginal benefit.

Griffin, Mary. Putting a price on information: practice illustrating a basic principle. (1980) Aslib Proceedings vol.42(1), p.26-34.

This paper describes the library and information department within Smiths Industries that operates services, including loans, acquisitions and periodicals, on a cost recovery basis. Griffin outlines example, expenditure and income details, and describes recording and charging procedures. She claims that this system offers a high degree of flexibility as there are no restrictions on what may be provided so long as users are prepared to pay for these services.

Griffiths, J M; King, D W. A manual of performance indicators for UK public libraries. (1989) King Research Ltd on behalf of the Office of Arts and Libraries. Unpublished draft.

This manual describes and develops a conceptual framework for the development of performance indicators for public libraries and applies the framework to a number of key public service areas.

Griffiths, J M; King D W. The contribution of on line database services to the productivity of their users. (1986) 10th On Line Information Meeting. Learned Information, p.69-76.

This paper summarises a four year research study, the aim of which is to establish monetary values for the benefits of scientific and technological reading. The authors attempt to do this by correlating input costs with a series of output indicators. Claims of global savings of $300 billion per annum are made as a result of this reading but from this brief presentation it is not entirely clear how this sum has been calculated.

Haley, R I. Benefit segmentation: a decision oriented research pool. (July 1968) Journal of Marketing vol.32, p.30-35.

According to this article most techniques of market segmentation rely on descriptive factors pertaining to purchasers and are not efficient predictors of future buyer behaviour. The author proposes an approach whereby market segments are delineated first on the basis of factors with a causal relationship to future purchase behaviour. The belief underlying this segmentation strategy is that the benefits which people are seeking in consuming a given product are the basic reasons for the existence of true market segments.

Hannabus, S. Measuring the value and marketing the service: an approach to library benefit. (October 1983) Aslib Proceedings vol.35(10), p.419-427.

The value of libraries and information services lies in their contribution to customer information needs. As non profit organisations this benefit is seen less as profit than benefit or utility to the communities they serve.

Hardy, M; Yeoh, J W; Crawford, S. Evaluating the impact of library services on the quality and cost of medical care. (January 1985) Bulletin Medical Library Association vol.73(1), p.43-46.

Changes in hospital funding have put pressure on hospital libraries to justify their existence. Such questions as did the libraries save lives or reduce the length of hospitalisation are now being asked. The authors review some positive approaches to these questions.

Hayes, R M; Pollack, A M; Nordhaus, S. An application of the Cobb-Douglas model to the Association of Research Libraries. (Fall 1983) Library and Information Science Research vol.5(3), p.291-325.

The Cobb-Douglas production function is an econometric model which relates three variables: measure of production, measures of capital investment and measures of labour. Production measures used were numbers of interlibrary loans, number of PhDs graduated, numbers of faculty and number of papers written. Labour measures were number of reader services staff and number of faculty. Capital included size of library and indexes of library ranks and sizes drawn from the Association of Research Library data. Various tables using the Cobb-Douglas formulae are presented in the paper.

Hernon, Peter; McClure, Charles R. Unobtrusive testing and library reference services. (1987a) Norwood, New Jersey, Ablex Publishing, 240p.

The authors present a comprehensive review of unobtrusive testing. Their objectives are to: place unobtrusive testing in the context of reference service evaluation; assess the correct answer fill rate as a performance measure; refine unobtrusive testing as an evaluation methodology; explore new applications of unobtrusive testing; encourage ongoing evaluation of reference services, discuss the impact of selected findings on larger issues of library management and education; identify additional research areas involving the use of unobtrusive testing.

Their conclusions, based on their own and other unobtrusive tests, suggest that academic and public library reference services typically achieve only a 55% correct answer fill rate. The view the authors portray therefore is one of reference services in crisis. Hernon and McClure claim the situation as they perceive it must be tackled by continuous programmes of evaluation using unobtrusive and other performance measures, the development of managerial strategies to act upon the results obtained, and co-operation with library schools to provide programmes of continuing education.

Hernon's and McClure's conclusions on the efficacy of unobtrusive testing are challenged for example by Childers, Bailey and Schumacher (all 1987). Reservations as to the validity of this technique emphasise the reliance of unobtrusive tests on factual type questions and suggest that results may not be applicable to all aspects of the reference process.

Hernon, Peter; McClure, Charles R. Contributions to, Library Reference Service: an unrecognised crisis - a Symposium. (1987b) The Journal of Acacemic Librarianship vol.13(2), p.69-71.

Introduction to a debate on the state of reference services as revealed by the authors use of unobtrusive testing, which they claim consistently show that only around 55% of test questions are answered fully and accurately.

Hernon, Peter; McClure, Charles R. Where do we go from here? A final response. (1987c) Contribution to, The Continuing Debate on Library Reference Service: a Mini-Symposium, The Journal of Academic Librarianship vol.13(5), p.282-284.

The authors acknowledge the limitation of unobtrusive testing, but they deny these invalidate the general conclusions and stress that the technique is only one of a range of methods which can usefully contribute to performance evaluation.

Hernon, Peter; McClure, Charles R. Quality of data issues in unobtrusive testing of library reference service: recommendations and strategies. (1987d) Library & Information Science Research vol.9(2), April-June p.77-93.

The authors discuss issues relating to the reliability, validity, utility and information 'value' of unobtrusive testing. They provide practical suggestions for improving the quality of the technique and identify topics for further methodological refinement. Study findings are also applied to library decision making and planning.

Note

Abbreviated abstract only because copy of paper not available until after the closing date for the completion of this bibliography.

Ifidon, S E. The evaluation of performance. (1986) Libri vol.36(3), p.224-229.

The author reviews performance evaluation and emphasises the need for clear objectives. He specifically comments on collection evaluation using expert lists to check on quality of the collection and assesses document delivery. He argues that the evaluative process should include the appraisal of library staff and the article contains a 17 point check list on staff qualities.

Kates, J R. One measure of a library's contribution. (Aug 1974) Special Libraries, p.332-336.

A study was undertaken to determine how many of the references cited in company publications were obtained by the library. Library use was also assessed and it was concluded that this detailed examination of citations and usage demonstrated that the library was closely allied to the activities of the company.

Kania, Antoinette M. Academic library standards and performance measures. (1988) College & Research Libraries vol.49(1), p.16-23.

Examines existing standards of the seven US regional accreditation commissions and demonstrates that these vary in length, style and content. Kania concludes that the focus of these standards is still based on inputs and processes rather than output measures. Kania suggests a model set of qualitative performance-oriented academic library standards.

Kania, Antoinette M. Performance measures for academic libraries: a twenty year perspective. (1988) New York, US Department of Education, Educational Resources Information Center Report, 8p.

A brief introduction is included with this bibliography which includes unannotated references on measures of access, user and users; techniques of collection evaluation; and assessments of reference services.

Kantor Paul B. Objective performance measures for academic and research libraries. (1984) Association of Research Libraries.

The Association of Research Libraries tested four measures in a group of libraries and the results of these tests are reported in this report. The measures tested were availability and accessibility of library materials, analyses of user activity, and assessing delays in interlibrary loan delivery. The report includes reproductions of the forms used in the study together with full methodologic detail enabling other libraries to use these measures.

Kelly, Lauren. Budgeting in non-profit organisations. (1985) Drexel Library Quarterly vol.21(3), p.3-18.

The author provides a useful overview of budget formats and discusses the strengths and limitations of these to the overall budgeting and accounting process.

King, Donald W; Roderer, Nancy K; Olsen, Harold A. Key papers in the economics of information. (1984) White Plains, NY, Knowledge Industry Publications, 372p.

This book attempts to bring together a selection of important articles which address various aspects of the economics of information. Part one covers the economic cost of information products and services; part two pricing, and the third part involves the benefit aspect of economic analysis of products and services. Some of the contributions provide a theoretical economic basis for information, while others discuss and describe methods, models and empirical results of economic analysis. Each of these sections is preceded by a short discussion, as well as an abstract and commentary on each of the articles.

King, J L; Schrems, E L. Cost benefit analysis in information systems development and operation in A reader on choosing an automated library system edited by J R Matthews. (1983) American Library Association, p.70-90.

This paper discusses cost benefit analysis as it is used in evaluating information system decisions in public and private organizations. It consists of a description of the nature and use of cost benefit analysis, the major techniques of such analyses and some key problems with cost benefit analysis as applied to information system evaluation.

King Research Inc. Performance measures for Oklahoma Public Libraries. (1982) Oklahoma State Department of Libraries.

A comprehensive project was launched to develop performance measures for Oklahoma City Libraries. The evaluation generated performance measures from internal statistics which included market penetration data. An availability survey was conducted and a 52% availability score was reported. A telephone survey was also conducted and full details are given of the procedure used to obtain representative samples. Full results of the study are included.

Koenig, Michael E D; Alperin, Victor. ZBB and PPBS: what's left now that the trendiness has gone? (1985) Drexel Library Quarterly vol.21(3), p.19-38.

Contains the report of a survey designed to show the impact of PPBS (Planning-Programming Budgeting System) and ZBB (Zero Based Budgeting) on libraries. The authors conclude that, although very few libraries follow either format, they predict the increase in the range of demands now placed on library budgets will once again focus attention upon alternative analysis techniques, including system analysis, operations research, cost-benefit analysis and program budgeting.

Kuehl, Philip G. Marketing viewpoints for user needs. (1973) in Economics of information dissemination: a symposium, edited by Robert S Taylor, Syracuse University.

Kuehl stresses the importance of classifying client communities according to relatively homogeneous use segments in order that library and information services can effectively respond to market needs.

LA Guidelines. Public and private sector relationships. (March 1987) Library Association Record vol.89(3), p.142-145.

Attempts to establish the principles which should determine the respective roles of the public and private sectors in the provision of library and information services. Reaffirms the obligation of the profession to protect and promote the rights of every individual to have free and equal access to sources of information without discrimination. The paper asserts that a certain level of stock and service should continue to be supported by the public purse. It does not rule out the option that some services could be charged at cost or to make a profit. The paper rejects the notion that any commercial services should be entirely left to the private sector.

Lancaster, F W. If you want to evaluate your library. (1988) Library Association, 193p.

This practical manual is largely an update and simplified version of Lancaster's earlier publication cited in this bibliography. The first half of the book is concerned with the evaluation of document delivery services and two chapters are devoted to the evaluation of reference and literature searching services.

Some of the chapters are somewhat superficial e.g. the ones devoted to buying versus borrowing cost effectiveness and cost benefit. Each chapter includes study questions as the book is intended for use within library schools.

Lancaster, F W. The measurement and evaluation of library services. (1977) Washington DC, Information Resources Press, 395p.

Conceived as a 'student textbook' Lancaster presents a critical survey and synthesis of the published literature on library evaluation. Following an overview of the concept of evaluation, Lancaster describes techniques for assessing catalogues, reference services, information retrieval services, library stock, document delivery, as well as technical services. Emphasis is placed on methodology, but the findings of practical studies are also described in order to demonstrate the type of results that have been achieved using various techniques. Lancaster himself admits, however, that his book is concerned only with how well a library satisfies what he regards as the tangible needs of its users. Indeed he deliberately excludes any consideration of the evaluation of libraries in terms of what Lancaster sees as their broader, but "largely unmeasurable 'benefits' to society".

Layard, Richard. Cost-benefit analysis. (1972) Harmondsworth, Penguin Books, 496p.

This is a collection of significant contributions to the theory and practice of cost benefit analysis. The book contains a very useful introduction to the subject by Layard himself. Subsequent papers deal with survey of cost benefit analysis, measurement techniques such as shadow pricing, and the value of time, the treatment of risk and income distributions, and concludes with a case study on the choice of location for a third London airport.

Layzell-Ward, P. (ed) Performance measures: a bibliography. (1982) Centre for Library and Information Management and Public Libraries Research Group.

This bibliography is concerned with performance measurement and its application within library systems and consists of some 220 English language items. All references are annotated with critical abstracts and the bibliography includes an author index.

Lewis, Dennis A. Today's challenge - tomorrow's choice: change or be changed or the doomsday scenario Mk 2. (1980) Journal of Information Science vol.2(2), p.59-74.

In this paper the author reviews the trends, including technological, financial and economical, social and behavioural, as well as managerial, which he says point to the likely demise of the information professional by the year 2,000. He then outlines the options for change and the actions which must be taken in order to avert this so-called 'doomsday scenario'.

Line, Maurice B. Library surveys - an introduction to the use, planning procedure and presentation of surveys. (1982) 2nd ed, revised by Sue Stone, London, Clive Bingley, 162p.

Intended as an introduction to the subject of library surveys this book is a useful starting point for practitioners who are considering conducting a survey, or who are seeking a better understanding of the surveys of others. The book is therefore arranged to help the reader through the survey process with a chapter devoted to the purpose and uses of library surveys, followed by sections on planning, data collection, analysis and the interpretation and presentation of results.

Line, Maurice B. Draft definitions - information and library needs, wants, demands and uses. (1974) vol.(2), p.87.

According to Line, the literature on 'user needs' has been confused by imprecision in terminology. In this short paper Line attempts to rectify this by offering a set of definitions covering needs, wants, demands and use.

Lynch, Mary Jo. Measurement of public library activity - the search for practical methods. (1983) Wilson Library Bulletin vol.57(5), p.388-393.

This paper traces the involvement of the US Public Library Association in the search to develop practical methods to measure services, and describes the philosophy behind the production of the PLA's manual on output measures (see Zweizig and Roderer 1982).

McClure, Charles R. A view from the trenches: costing and performance measures for academic library public services. (1986) College and Research Libraries vol.47, p.323-336.

Author conducted a survey of attitudes of librarians in US academic libraries towards performance measurement. The survey suggests that respondents have little faith in the utility of cost data and performance measures, that such information rarely has much impact on decision taking, that in house data frequently lacks validity and reliability and that libraries are too understaffed to take time away from the provision of services to identify, collect and analyse such data.

McClure, Charles R et al. Planning and role setting for public libraries - a manual of options and procedures. (1987) Chicago, American Library Association, 117p.

Revised edition of the practical planning manual sponsored by the Public Library Association of the American Library Association (see Palmour, Vernon E et al, 1980). This manual introduces the concept of role setting into the planning process. The authors emphasise the importance of the relationship between a library's roles and the needs and expectations of the community it serves. Librarians are encouraged to focus on library service profiles or "roles" which are most appropriate to serve these local needs. Like its predecessor the manual is intended to be a step-by-step guide through the process of reviewing existing conditions and services, defining a library's roles and mission, setting goals and objectives, choosing strategies to achieve the objectives, and evaluating the results of the planning process.

McClure, Charles R; Hernon, Peter. Unobtrusive testing and the role of library management. (1987) Reference Librarian 18 (Summer 87), p.71-88.

The authors discuss the development of strategies to review and improve reference services on a regular basis. Also describe managerial responsibilities regarding the use of unobtrusive testing. Abbreviated abstract only because copy of paper not available until after the closing date for the completion of this bibliography.

McClure, Charles R; Zweizig, Douglas L; Van House, Nancy A; Lynch, Mary Jo. Output measures myths, realities and prospects. (1986) Public Libraries vol.25(2), p.49-52

This paper reviews some of the criticisms levelled at the Public Library Association sponsored output measures for public libraries embodied in the manual provided by Zweizig and Rodger in 1982. The authors reaffirm their belief in the general utility of output measures as one of a number of possible indicators of performance evaluation. They do however outline a number of suggestions for the future development of these output measures.

McClure, Charles R; Reifsnyder, B. Performance measures for corporate information centers. (July 1984) Special Libraries vol.75(3), p.193-204

Authors maintain that performance measures developed in the public library domain can be applied to special libraries. Performance techniques reviewed include means of assessing library awareness, market penetration approaches and quality of information support services.

McElroy, A Rennie. Library information services evaluation: a case history. (May 1982) Pharmaceutical R & D vol.34(5), p.249-265.

This paper describes a 19 week project which sought to evaluate the totality of library services at a major pharmaceutical company. A number of approaches were used in the project including user ranking of services; assessments of stock utilization; user interviews; budget gaming exercises where users were asked how they would spend additional library funds; assessments of current awareness services and derived value calculations. The author includes an analysis of the costs of the evaluative exercise.

Manthey, Teresa; Brown, Jeanne Owen. Evaluating a special library using public library measures. Special Libraries (1985) vol.76(4), p.282-289.

The paper relates an attempt to apply the PLA output measures to a hospital library. Of the 12 measures outlined, 6 were found to be applicable to the hospital, and an additional 4 were considered to have been possibly useful to other special libraries. This paper does however clearly illustrate the limitations of these type of output measures. Generally the analysis of the figures raised more questions than it answered. For example circulation per capita did nothing to explain the value of the collection to various segments of the client community; reference transactions per capita did not explain why one group asked for fewer reference questions than others; and reference fill rate showed the percentage of reference questions answered promptly but did not provide any clue as to the accuracy or value of the answers given. This paper showed the need for further in-depth evaluation studies in order to perhaps provide answers to these questions. The authors themselves conclude that the questions generated as a result of the measurement process proved to be more valuable than the actual figures produced.

Mishan, E J. Cost benefit analysis - an informal introduction. (1988) 4th ed, London, Unwin Hyman, 461p.

The latest revision of a standard yet thorough introduction to the subject of cost benefit analysis. This book contains a useful discussion on the economic concepts of costs and benefits, including for example an analysis of consumers' surplus and shadow pricing.

Moffatt, Michael. Interlibrary comparison in Do we really need libraries? (1983) Proceedings of the first joint Library Association Cranfield Institute of Technology Conference on performance, edited by J Blagden, Cranfield, Cranfield Press, p.97-111.

In his paper the author gives a brief introduction to the philosophy of interfirm comparisons and describes the work of the Centre for Interfirm Comparison. He attempts to outline the value of this technique for providing comparative data on the resources used by libraries and the ways in which those resources have been used to provide the necessary functions and services. By enabling the calculation of unit costs for each activity it is hoped that interlibrary comparison will reveal for example why a library might have proportionally higher unit costs than another for a particular activity or function.

The discussion that follows the presentation itself raises a number of points which appear to question the validity of the technique. These include reservations concerning the possible misuse or misinterpretation of the data; inconsistencies in data collection techniques and output measures between the participating libraries make it difficult to guarantee that like data is in fact being compared; the existence of other factors such as organisation structure, geographical location and history all affect outcomes while the comparison provides no indication of service quality; and finally it was questioned whether the results obtained justified the outlay in time and resources expended by the libraries involved in these comparisons. The author himself suggests that interlibrary comparison must be seen as a tool for producing information which can be helpful to librarians as part of a more detailed evaluation of their own particular services.

National Consumer Council. Measuring up, paper 3, Public Libraries. (1986)

The Council generally wishes to see greater consumer involvement in setting priorities for local government services in general and library services in particular. Technique used in the fieldwork conducted at Newcastle and Cambridge included the use of checklists, group discussion with users and non users, and simple surveys of users exiting from public libraries. The results of these 'exit polls' show a high level of satisfaction with the service with 95% of respondents evincing some level of satisfaction. The NCC admit however that their survey technique was flawed in that they requested generalised assessments of satisfaction which may have masked specific causes of dissatisfaction. The report provides a useful introduction to the whole arena of performance evaluation and drew attention to the problem of defining catchment areas in order to assess take up of service.

Newcastle upon Tyne, City of, Performance Review and Efficiency Skills Committee. First use of public services and consumer attitudes to the local authority in Newcastle. (1985) West City Consumer Survey.

The subjective perceptions of a service or of a feature of local authority activity bear no necessary connection to that service or authority objective, performance, efficiency or success. A good service by any objective standard might forever be unfavourably perceived because expectations are inappropriate. Indeed some services might never be perceived favourably, eg statutory aspects of child care.

Norton, Bob. Charging for library and information services. (1988) Viewpoints in LIS 1, Library Association.

The author reviews the arguments for and against charging in the public sector. He maintains that libraries are being driven towards charging albeit selectively by the demand for new expensive services driven by new technology and because library budgets are shrinking in real terms.

Office of Arts and Libraries. Record of an oral statement made by the Minister for the Arts on 8 February 1989 [to the House of Commons]. (1989) Office of Arts and Libraries, 4p.

Indicates that local authorities will be allowed to contract out services but they will remain responsible for the nature and quality of that service. Defines which services library authorities can charge for but all such charges will be discretionary.

Office of Arts and Libraries. Financing our public library service: four subjects for debate - a consultative paper presented to Parliament by the Minister for the Arts. (1988) CM 324, London, HMSO, 21p.

The proposals contained in this green paper represent the most significant change in government approach to public libraries since the 1964 Act. It affirms the commitment to the maintenance of a free 'basic library service', but proposes economic pricing, contracting out, competitive tendering and joint ventures with the private sector.

Office of Arts and Libraries. A costing system for public libraries. A model developed by Cipfa Services Ltd, (1987) London, HMSO, Library Information Series No.17, 33p.

This report sets our a model costing system for public libraries based on an examination of existing practises in library authorities. It includes the results of a practical study to relate the costing framework to the library services of the London Borough of Croydon. It attempts to establish standardised procedures for producing information on library service costs compared with budget heads and sub-heads; library service costs allocated to cost centres using a standard form of analysis, costs analysed by function areas and, data permitting, the calculation of a range of unit costs including issues, acquisitions, opening hours, etc, as well as income generation. The framework on its own however does not provide for an evaluation of the quality of the services offered but has been devised in such a way as to facilitate the inclusion of additional and more sophisticated measures of performance when these are available.

Office of Arts and Libraries. Joint enterprise: roles and relationships of the public and private sectors in the provision of library and information services. (1987) Library Information Series No.16, London, HMSO, 49p.

Report of a Library and Information Services Council and British Library Research and Development Department Working Party on the potential scope for the development of greater interaction between public and private sectors in the provision of library and information services.

Oldman, Christine M. The value of academic libraries: a methodological investigation. (1978) Cranfield Institute of Technology, School of Management, PhD thesis.

This thesis is concerned with the empirical examination of methods for measuring value provided by library and information services. The study focuses on the academic libraries at Cranfield and at Loughborough University, and explores the interaction between the libraries and their client communities. It reports on the findings of a number of attitudinal surveys which explore how users' initial perceptions and expectations of a library changed over a period of time when the libraries were actually used. The objective of the study is to show how the library manager can better understand the contribution made by library and information services to the work and goals of the organisation in order to facilitate resource management and allocation decisions. The author concludes that a user oriented approach to evaluation can usually lead to more effective management of resources.

Orr, Richard H. Measuring the goodness of library services: a general framework for considering quantitative measures. (1973) Journal of Documentation vol.29, p.315-332.

The paper presents a general conceptual framework for considering the relative advantages and disadvantages of qualitative and quantitative measures of library effectiveness. A milestone paper in that the author distinguished between how good the library is and how much good the library does.

Orr, Richard H et al. Development of methodologic tools for planning and managing library services: I Project goals and approach (1968) Bulletin of the Medical Library Association vol.56(3), p.235-240.

Orr, Richard H et al. Development of methodologic tools for planning and managing library services. II Measuring a library's capability for providing documents. (1968) Bulletin of the Medical Library Association vol.56(3), p.241-267.

Orr, Richard H et al. Development of methodologic tools for planning and managing library services. III Standardized inventories of library services. (1968) Bulletin of the Medical Library Association vol.56(4), p.380-403.

Together these three articles describe stages in the development of a methodology designed to assess a library's ability to deliver known documents. The first article discusses the conceptual framework of the project. In the second part the authors provide an account of a library test to determine how long would be required for users to obtain these documents. The series concludes with a description of a standardized procedure for eliciting those details of a library's service policies that are important to its users. It also includes a method for weighting the data to reflect the relative desirability of different policies so that it is possible to see how a library's policies compare with those of an 'optimal' library. It should be noted that a fourth paper which presents a selective bibliography to encourage the development of more efficient and effective services appeared in a later issue of the same journal. The full reference is Orr, Richard A. Development of methodologic tools for planning and managing library services: IV Bibliography of studies selected for methods and data useful to biomedical libraries. (1970) Bulletin of the Medical Library Association vol.58(3) p.350-377.

Owen, Amy. Output measures and state library development programs: a national survey. (1985) Public Libraries vol.24(3), p.98-101.

This article provides the results of a survey indicating the degree of involvement of each of the fifty US state libraries in output measurement. Responses fall into several categories: states not using the resources; states emphasising continuing education or consultancy to promote local use of output measures; states using output measures in connection with a single library development program; states using output measures in an integrated program that ties together two or more development activities.

Palmour, Vernon E; Bellassai, Marcia C; De Wath, Nancy V. A planning process for public libraries. (1980) Chicago. American Library Association, 1980, 304pp.

This manual developed out of a decision by the Public Library Association of the American Library Association that standards for public libraries should be determined at local level and should be based on an analysis of the community a library serves, the library's current range of services and the opinion of a planning committee about the goals and objectives of the library and its role in the local community. The manual describes a five year planning cycle which begins with the library developing and implementing a long-range library plan. The initial planning process is followed by continuous cycles which monitor and evaluate progress towards goals, review and update goals, objectives and priorities, develop and evaluate new strategies if required, and implement these new strategies. At the end of the five year cycle a new planning committee begins a total re-assessment of the library role and goals, so that planning becomes a continuous process.

The manual does offer criteria on which to evaluate library services, but recommends that library managers set their own performance criteria and objectives according to local circumstances. The information is to be provided from a needs assessment of the local community using secondary sources and primary data gathered from surveys. Although the manual does provide advice on the collection of both input and output measures, subsequent experience revealed inconsistencies in data collection and analysis methods. The need to provide a more consistent and simplified approach to this led to the publication of the PLA manual on output measures (see Zweizig and Roger, 1982).

Powell, Ronald R. The relationship of library user studies to performance measures: a review of the literature. (Jan 1988) Illinois University, Graduate School of Library and Information Science, Occasional Papers Number 181.

Arguing that user studies and performance measures provide two major approaches to evaluating the effectiveness of library services, this occasional paper presents an overview of the literature, examines the goals and approaches in user studies and performance measures, and provides suggestions for increasing the potential benefits of both by combining the two techniques. The resulting approach - performance measures based on user studies - is then discussed in terms of data collection, possible benefits, and limitations. It is concluded that: (1) valid procedures, i.e. measures that actually measure what they purport to measure, must be utilized by libraries to adequately evaluate their services; (2) libraries should be most concerned with measuring their ultimate product, performance or effectiveness, based on user data such as satisfaction; (3) a real need exists for libraries to be accountable for the effectiveness of their services; and (4) user-oriented performance measures provide a valid evaluation technique. (A 181-item reference list concludes the document.)

Ralli, Tony. Performance measures for academic libraries. (1987) Academic and Research Library vol.18, p.1-9.

A brief review of the reasons for measuring performance together with an assessment of the document delivery and collection evaluation techniques.

Ramsing, K D; Wish, J R. What do library users want? A conjoint measurement technique may yield the answer. (1982) Information Processing and Management vol.18(5), p.237-242.

Outlines a more systematic approach using conjoint analysis to determine what users want especially when there are different ways of delivering a particular service. Illustrates the use of the technique in a study of users preferences for online and manual searching.

Ratchford, B T. Cost benefit models for explaining consumer choice and information seeking behavior. (February 1982) Management Science vol.28(2), p.197-212.

This paper is concerned with the information seeking behaviour of potential purchasers of consumer goods. Although the focus is not directly relevant to the information and library environment some interesting hypotheses are suggested. These include (i) consumers will always be attempting to develop effective trade-offs between searching for more information to improve purchase decisions and the cost of so doing (ii) information seeking can produce carry-over benefits outside the specific transaction for which the search is conducted (iii) high salary earners will be concerned to save their time and will thus value highly intermediaries and published sources that enable them to achieve this.

Revill, D H. Availability as a performance measure for academic libraries. (January 1987) Journal of Librarianship vol.19(1), p.14-30.

Measures of availability are advocated as performance indicators for libraries within higher education and for the purposes of inter library comparison. Previous work is reviewed both in terms of results achieved and methods used. The method employed in the author's own library (Liverpool Polytechnic) is described. The results show a high degree of availability.

Roberts, Stephen A. Cost management for library and information services. (1985) London. Butterworths.

The author begins by noting the relatively weak development of financial and management accounting systems in libraries compared to conventional business enterprises. He argues that with increasing economic financial pressures on libraries and the growth in the number of library services, or parts of them, which are orientated to profit making, or at least cost recovery, library managers must adopt a more rigorous approach to cost management. He stresses the need for the development of management information systems in which budgeting, accounting and performance measurement systems are related. Detailed line by line or even programme budgets provide information on financial inputs but do not provide throughput and output cost data necessary for effective control and performance evaluation. Roberts suggests that cost measurement is a necessary condition for the development of performance measures. He describes methods for cost study categorisation, calculation and measurement, and discusses some specific issues and problems involved in the implementation of cost collection programmes. In bringing together the themes of budgeting, accounting, costing and performance measurement, Roberts outlines in practical terms the form which a library based management information system might take, and makes suggestions on how library managers might begin to experiment with the concepts of management information in their own systems. He concludes by attempting to illustrate these principles by reference to an illustrated model of an imaginary information service. Overall the book constitutes a useful practical guide to cost study, and is intended to provoke renewed interest in a previously comparatively neglected area of library management technique.

Roberts, Stephen A. Costing and the economics of library and information services. (1984) London, Aslib, 347p.

This reader brings together a collection of some of the more important contributions to the study of costing and management accounting for libraries. The papers have been carefully selected by the editor to provide a progression from the cost analysis to the economic analysis of library operations. Four of the book's five sections include papers which are broadly concerned with methods of cost data collection, cost analysis and management accounting. The concluding section focuses on the development of a body of economic theory relevant to libraries, in which cost data is seen to play a significant part. In bringing together a number of papers already perhaps well known to those familiar with the literature of library costing and economics, this reader covers well documented territory. Nevertheless each section is preceded by a commentary by the editor which serves to underline the context of the papers. Moreover this collection clearly identifies the themes which Roberts himself has explored further in his subsequent monograph (see above for abstract).

Robson, A P. Essential accounting for managers. (1988) 5th ed, London, Cassell, 122p.

This is a standard introduction to the essentials of modern management accounting and is aimed at a wide variety of managers who have to deal with accountants and accounting in practice.

Rodger, Elizabeth M. The evaluation of library and information services in terms of economic restraint: the university view. (Nov/Dec 1987) Aslib Proceedings vol.39(11/12), p.349-354.

Reviews a number of intermediate measures of effectiveness such as costs of interlibrary loans, hours of opening and comparisons of books purchased in different subjects with numbers borrowed.

Rosenberg, Philip. Cost funding for public libraries: a managers handbook. (1985) Chicago, American Library Association, 95p.

This manual is one of a series of publications sponsored by the Public Library Association of the American Library Association in recent years which aim to offer practical advice and encouragement to library managers on various aspects of planning and evaluation. It describes five basic steps for the isolation and estimation of costs associated with a particular library activity. These are:

deciding on a cost centre; identifying appropriate cost centre activities and tasks; selecting units of measure; determining the steps involved in collecting unit cost information; analysing the data. Note the manual does not recommend which library activities should be costed or set firm rules on how to select cost centres for a particular library. The emphasis of the manual is to encourage the integration of cost data into the general management process, and thus it concludes with a discussion of the applications of cost data.

Rout, R K. Measuring users satisfaction: a quantitative model. (March 1982) Iaslic Bulletin vol.27(1), p.1-8.

A general view of performance assessment is presented in which an outline of an attempt to quantify user attitudes towards various library services is given.

Schauer, Bruce P. The economics of managing library service. (1986) Chicago, American Library Association, 278p.

The book examines microeconomics and its application to library management problems. In part one the author presents the central theoretical apparatus of microeconomics as a foundation for analysing the behaviour of libraries and their users. He suggests that microeconomic analysis will enable library managers to predict what may happen to use when the mix of inputs into a service is varied. Thus choices relating to the allocation of funds can be based on the predicted added cost and added benefit of alternative courses of action. The second half of the book is devoted to some of the more important elements involved in quantitative decision models. It begins with an introductory chapter on probability theory and then goes on to illustrate practical applications of probability and economic reasoning. Decision theory and cost-benefit approaches are used to evaluate library based projects such as new buildings and security systems. There is a concluding chapter on public library finance with particular reference to the implications of pricing for library services. The focus of the book is therefore very much on theoretical analysis rather than a description or investigation of the experience of existing library services.

Schumacher, Mark. A view from the trenches. Contribution to The Continuing Debate on Library Reference Service, a Mini-Symposium. (1987) Journal of Academic Librarianship vol.13(5), p.278-279.

This article is a contribution to the debate on the validity of unobtrusive testing, Inspired particularly by the work of Hernon and McClure (1987). This, as with the contribution of Bailey (1987), presents the views of a practicing reference librarian.

Seff, Laura J. Management uses of output measures at branch and systems level in Baltimore County public library. (1987) Public Libraries vol.26(3), p.120-122.

The author reports that attempts to use output measures as fundamental indicators of success in reaching selected objectives appeared fruitless when projected increases fell within the margin of error for the library's sample size. However Seff comments that the process of analysing the measures has been more useful than the numbers themselves. The analysis has provided a wealth of information which has been helpful to the library management and planning process. Examples given include an analysis of patron requests, which enabled the library to make the acquisition of duplicate copies more responsive to user demand, and this possibly contributed to a sizeable overall increase in circulation; document delivery figures suggested improvements to reserves procedures; and the high referred rate in a reference file survey indicated training priorities to improve reference services.

Shohan, Snunith. A cost-preference study of the decentralization of academic library services. (1982) Library Research 4(2), p.175-194.

This paper explores a marginal cost approach to infer the costs incurred because a library service is provided through a branch library rather than through a central library. Marginal costs are considered as those arising solely from the fact that the library is a branch, including the cost of duplicating administration and materials, etc. It was found that labour costs resulting from decentralisation were significant, but not the additional costs of materials. The results of a user survey indicated that there was a preference for the existing convenient branch, even to the prospect of using costs savings for additional services with centralised provision. Benefits arising from the branch library were regarded as being accessibility, the involvement of the faculty in library policy, a more flexible loan policy and greater personal attention from staff. The author concludes therefore that user preference for a branch library may be economically valid if all costs are considered. However, in attempting a cost-preference rather than a rigourous cost-benefit analysis, the author makes little attempt to quantify these benefits. Moreover marginal costs are confined to an analysis of labour and materials and no attempt is made to quantify additional costs such as space, equipment and maintenance charges.

Silvey, Robert. In Where ratings don't rule by Robert M Worcester. (1976) Observer, 11 April, p.19-22.

Although this article is concerned with broadcasting its central theme that a programme's success should not be measured by the absolute size of the audience as much as by how nearly it approaches the size of its intended or targeted audience is a concept which can usefully be applied to assessing the market penetration of a library or information service.

Smith, B B. Marketing strategies for libraries. (1983) Library Management vol.4(1), p.1-52.

This comprehensive review introduces a wide range of marketing concepts and techniques and suggests ways as to how these might be applied in public libraries. The review includes definitions of marketing terms, market analysis, consumer analysis including segmentation, market research, product analysis, distribution, and promotion. An extensive bibliography is appended to the review.

Sparrow, Elizabeth. Management information in the British Library Humanities and Social Sciences Division. (1988) Journal of Librarianship vol.20(2), p.94-107.

This article describes how performance indicators are being evolved in the British Library Humanities and Social Sciences Division.

Stone, S. Interlibrary loans: a study of antecedents and outcomes of interlibrary loan requests. (1983) CRUS Occasional Paper No.7. Centre for Research on User Studies.

This study examined knowledge that users had of requested items before making an interlibrary loan request and the expectation that users had of the requested items utility. The users were questioned again as to how useful the documents supplied were and 70% of the supplied requests appeared to be satisfactory. The survey suggests that users might be more successful in identifying appropriate materials if they made greater use of abstracting services. The survey also discovered many cases where the items delivered were more relevant or useful than originally expected.

Suchman, Edward. Evaluative research: principles and practices in public service and social action programs. (1967) Russel Sage Foundation.

This is a useful introduction to the methodology of evaluation based on experience drawn from studies in the public and social services.

Taylor, R S. Value-added process in information systems. (1986) Ablex Publishing Corporation.

The author presents a model of the information process consisting of the system, value, value-added and information outputs. The author applies these concepts and this model to how value is added in libraries, abstracting and indexing services, information analysis and information in decision making. He also explores the relationship of information to productivity and emphasises the importance of assessing who is using the service with what effect.

Thompson, James. The end of libraries. (1983) Electronic Library vol.1(4), p.245-255.

In this deliberately provocative article Thompson warns of the threats facing the profession from the organisational and financial impasse of conventional libraries and the advent of new technology for storage, handling and transmission of information that will eventually displace the book as the centre of mankind's 'communal memory'. He argues that librarians must grasp the opportunities offered by this technology or face the possibility of some future extinction.

Thompson, Jan. Unobtrusive reference service testing at Auckland public library. (1987) New Zealand Libraries vol.45(6), p.117-119.

This paper begins with a brief review of previous unobtrusive surveys and then describes the experience at Aukland. In terms of results the Aukland survey very much reflects results achieved elsewhere in that 56% of questions correctly answered, 18% partially correctly, 14.5% were referred, 7% incorrectly answered and 4.5% no answer or referral given. The author concludes with a note on the ethics of unobtrusive testing, but is in no doubt as to its value stating that "if another technique could give us the same information about the information services provided in libraries it would be preferred, but none as effective has been found".

Totterdell, Barry; Bird, Jean. The effective library: report of the Hillingdon Project on Public Library Effectiveness. (1976) edited by Margaret Redfern, London, Library Association, 207p.

The report of a project to develop a methodology for measuring the effectiveness of public library services within a given community. The authors discuss the concept of need, output measures are described and analyses are presented of data gathered from surveys of branch libraries in three areas of Hillingdon. These results show that there is little difference between users and non users in their attitude towards public libraries, and these are characterised by generally low expectations of services.

Van House, Nancy A et al. Output measures for public libraries - a manual of standardised procedures. (1987) Chicago, American Library Association, 99p.

Revised edition of the manual sponsored by the Public Library Association of the American Library Association (see Zweizig and Rodger 1982) which incorporates a number of the methodological enhancements which arose out of the analysis following the publication of the earlier work.

Van House, Nancy A; Childers Thomas. Unobtrusive evaluation of a reference referral network. The California experience. (1984) Library and Information Science Research vol.6(3), p.305-319.

This study is of interest because, whereas previous unobtrusive studies have measured reference service at the point of contact with the end-user, this investigation sought to determine the performance of non-public units (ie in California questions not answered at a local level can be referred on to either of two state level reference centers) of a large reference referral network. From a methodological viewpoint this particular study is also unusual because of its reliance on pre-existing records of reference transactions, for in the California referral networks written documentation is available for the vast majority of the questions handled. This study also involved the use of an external panel of experienced reference librarians to independently verify the accuracy of the answers given. In terms therefore of the size and complexity of the study, and its dependence on the availability of written records, it is perhaps doubtful that this method, however interesting from the viewpoint of its findings, could be of general applicability.

Vickery, B C. Information systems. (1973) London, Butterworths, 350p.

In a pioneering work on information transfer Vickery attempts to develop a systems approach for the study of a wide range of library and information activities. While the emphasis of the book is very much on information retrieval there are chapters on information use, the identification of components of information systems, as well as procedures for the analysis and modeling of these systems. Concluding chapters focus on the design and evaluation of information systems and include a useful discussion on the concepts of effectiveness, efficiency and value.

Vickery, B C; Vickery, A. Information science in theory and practice. (1987) London, Butterworths, 384p.

This book attempts to present and discuss a scientific understanding of the process of information transfer. Although the impact of new technology is explored, the authors emphasise the process of information transfer as a human social activity. As a result the book contains both a discussion of human behaviour in information transfer as well as an examination of information systems. The authors also discuss the importance of evaluating information systems in terms of how well they are meeting the needs, wants and demands of their intended recipients, and whether these results are being achieved in an economic fashion.

Virgo, Julie A C. Costing and pricing information services. (1985) Drexel Library Quarterly vol.21(3), p.75-98.

Virgo outlines the steps involved in costing information services and discusses the use of cost data for price setting in making informed management decisions and for communicating more effectively with funding bodies.

Warden, C L. User evaluation of a corporate online search service. (April 1981) Special Libraries vol.172(2) p.113-117.

The responses to an evaluation questionnaire administered primarily to first time and remote-site users of a corporate online search service indicated that the searches yeild a high percentage of relevant citations for most users. The study also claimed that significant savings of users' time was achieved through use of online search facilities.

Webb, Eugene J et al. Unobtrusive measures: non-reactive research in the social sciences. (1966) Rand McNally.

Seminal investigation of research methods in the social sciences which presented unobtrusive testing as an alternative to survey tchniques which were based entirely on self-reporting.

Weech, Terry L; Goldhor, Herbert. Obtrusive versus unobtrusive evaluation of reference service in five Illinois public libraries: a pilot study. (1982). The Library Quarterly vol.52(4), p.305-324.

This article describes the results of a pilot study to determine the relative effectiveness of obtrusive and unobtrusive methods of evaluating library reference services. The authors concluded that the libraries performed slightly, but statistically significantly, better on the obtrusive test than on the unobtrusive one and suggest this provides at least partial confirmation of the biasing effect of obtrusive tests.

White, H S. Cost benefit analysis and other fun and games. (15 Feb 1985) Library Journal, p.118-121.

Explores and defines the concepts of cost effectiveness, cost efficiency and cost benefit analysis. Argues that cost benefit analysis cannot be applied to libraries because it is not possible to assess the alternative of closing the library. Is equally critical of judging a library on the degree of willingness to pay for services. Is also dubious of justifying a library on the basis of improved productivity because it rarely leads to realising the earnings by staff reductions.

Wilde, D U; Cooper, N R. Justifying your information center's budget. (1988) Proceedings of the 9th National Online Meeting, p.421-427.

This paper advocates an evaluative approach which involves the identification and reporting of specific examples in which information on technology supplied by the information centre encouraged new product development, cost reduction and other benefits to the company the center supports. An outline of the methodology is given which effectively captures the desired feedback without disrupting the work of the information centre.

Williams, Roy. An unobtrusive survey of academic library reference services. (1987) Library and Information Research News vol.10(37 & 38), p.12-40.

This paper describes the first unobtrusive test of academic library reference services in the UK. Williams' findings that in the 20 libraries tested correct answers were given in less than two out of three cases (64%) reveal much the same results as similar tests in the United States and in public libraries. He also concludes that there did not seem to be significant differences in performance between polytechnic and university libraries.

Williams, R V. Productivity measurements in special libraries: prospects and problems for use in performance evaluation. (Spring 1988) Special Libraries vol.79(2), p.101-114.

The author advocates the use of productivity measurement in libraries and compares the advantage of this technique with other approaches to performance measurement including cost benefit analysis, attitude studies, document delivery and qualitative analysis. Detailed results are given of productivity measurements in a number of US federal libraries.

Wills, G; Christopher, M. Cost benefit analysis of company information needs. (1970) Unesco Bulletin for Libraries vol.24(1), p.9-23.

The authors advocate the application of the technique of the expected value of perfect information (EVPI) in assessing expenditure on information for a new product launch. The EVPI technique uses Bayesian statistics to calculate the maximum that might be spent on information and defines information broadly to include for example the costs of market research. Useful technique for large scale projects with a heavy information input but not appropriate as a means of generally establishing investment levels in libraries.

Wolfe, James N et al. The economics of technical information systems. (1974) New York, Praeger, 167p.

The authors attempt to develop a general methodology for the evaluation of secondary information services located within a government department or business enterprise when the service is not sold at a price that covers its actual cost. The authors identify the main components of secondary information services as abstracts journals, titles listings, SDI services, and enquiry answering services. The study begins with a discussion of the theory and methodology of evaluation and the authors then describe a framework to assess the cost effectiveness of these secondary information services.

Zachert, M J; Williams, R V. Marketing measures for information services. (Spring 1986) Special Libraries vol.77(2), p.61-70.

This paper explores and synthesizes concepts drawn from the literature of marketing and performance evaluation. Potentially useful approaches to market structure analysis design, decision making and marketing programme evaluation are described.

Zweizig, Douglas L. So go figure: measuring library effectiveness. (1987) Public Libraries vol.26(1), p.21-24.

In this article the author discusses some of the evaluation issues and developments which have emerged since the publication of Output measures for public libraries: a manual of standardized procedures by Zweizig and Rodger (1982) (see below). Zweizig suggests that the evaluation should be seen as a way of providing information to improve performance rather than for making a final qualitative judgement as to the 'goodness' or 'badness' if a library service. He stresses the importance of avoiding over-ambitious evaluation programmes in order to concentrate on measures which are inexpensive to collect but which can contribute useful information to the management process.

Zweizig, Douglas L; Braune, Joan A; Waity, Gloria. Output measures for children's services in Wisconsin public libraries: a pilot project 1984-85. (1985) New York, US Department of Education. Educational Resources Information Centre Report.

Results from a pilot study to test the adaptations of the PLA sponsored output measures in a practical situation, i.e. the children's services in Wisconsin Public Libraries. It discusses measures used and data collection methods. The use of these measures does not indicate any qualitative judgements regarding the service studies.

Zweizig, Douglas; Rodger, Eleanor Jo. Output measures for public libraries. (1982) Chicago, American Library Association, 100p.

This practical manual was sponsored by the Public Library Association of the American Library Association as part of its attempt to move away from national public library standards towards a more local determination of library needs. Intended to reinforce and support the PLA's earlier planning manual (see Palmour, Vernon E. 1980) this publication was designed to provide libraries with consistent and standardised methods for collecting output information. The manual describes twelve output measures selected because they can be readily interpreted. The chapter headings describe the twelve types: circulation per capita, in-library materials use per capita, library visits per capita, program attendance per capita, reference transaction per capita, reference fill rate, title fill rate, subject and author fill rate, browsers' fill rate, registration as a percentage of population, turnover rate, and document delivery. Each chapter contains a definition of the measure, method of collection and suggested additional (level II) measures. Summary sheets for recording data are also provided.

Since its publication the manual has been the subject of considerable debate regarding the utility of the measures described. Among the criticisms levelled at it are that the techniques are too simplistic, they are prone to statistical error, they are concerned with quantitative rather than qualitative valuations of library output and they are affected by differences in user behaviour. See for example the work of D'Elia D and Rodger (1987) and D'Elia and Walsh (1985). Evidence from practical experience of using the measures suggests that the analysis is more helpful from a management information view point than for the statistics themselves, see for example Manthey and Brown (1985) and Seff (1987).